Designing for Performance

Learning Science, Microlearning, & AI-Supported Training That Works

DOROTHY BOULDRICK, DHA, MBA

ISBN: 979-8-9938024-0-4 (Paperback)

Acknowledgments

First and foremost, I give thanks to my Lord and Savior Jesus Christ, from whom all ideas and creativity flow. This work is a testament to the gifts He has graciously bestowed upon me.

This book would not have been possible without the unwavering support of many remarkable individuals who have walked alongside me throughout my career. To my colleagues, mentors, and students who have challenged me, inspired me, and deepened my understanding of education and instructional design, your influence permeates these pages in ways both seen and unseen.

To my family and special friend who offered encouragement during the writing of this book, who believed in me and never doubted that I could do this, I am deeply grateful for your love, encouragement and support.

A special thank you to 7taps for providing the images of my microlessons to share with my readers.

Contents

About the Author

Dr. Dorothy Bouldrick is an accomplished instructional designer, educator, and healthcare workforce learning & development strategist who advances healthcare education through digital learning and evidence-based practices. With over twenty-five years of experience in health administration, corporate education, higher education, and instructional design, she integrates learning science and technology to create impactful, learner-focused solutions.

Her credentials include a Postgraduate Certificate in Training to Teach in Medicine from Harvard Medical School, Doctor of Health Administration (DHA) from the Medical University of South Carolina (MUSC), an MBA from Webster University, and a B.S. in Organizational Management from Claflin University, Certified Kirkpatrick Performance Designer and a Certified Digital Learning Specialist.

As **Founder** and **Healthcare Workforce L&D Strategist** of **BouldVision LLC**™, she authors and designs digital learning interventions and consults nationally.

Dr. Bouldrick's experience includes roles as Medical Assisting Program Director, leading curriculum, accreditation, and faculty development, an Instructional Designer/Developer with Elsevier, creating digital learning solutions for nursing workforce development and Assistant Professor at Morehouse School of Medicine where she taught healthcare leadership development in the Doctor of Health Administration (DHA) program.

Her book, *Designing for Performance, Learning Science, Microlearning & AI-Supported Training That Works* presents The Four Pillars of Performance-Focused Learning™ she uses to improve workforce development and enhance real-world performance.

Introduction

Over the past twenty-five years, I have worked as a medical assisting program director, an instructional designer, an eLearning developer in corporate education, and an assistant professor in graduate healthcare programs. I have designed training for frontline clinical staff, healthcare executives, and everyone in between. I have watched brilliant content fail to change anything and simple interventions transform performance. The difference, I have learned, is not production quality or technological sophistication. The difference is knowing how people learn and design philosophy. Traditional instructional design asks: What information should learners receive? Performance design asks: What results must improve, what behaviors will produce those results, and how do we design learning that makes those behaviors automatic?

This shift from content delivery to performance improvement changes everything. It changes what questions you ask stakeholders. It changes how you storyboard, author content, design screens and develop in eLearning. It changes how you structure assessments. It changes what you measure and what you consider success. Most importantly, it changes the impact you have on your organization and the people you serve.

Why This Book, Why Now

The learning and development landscape is evolving rapidly. The Workforce Wishlist 2025 report from upGrad Enterprise confirmed what many of us have observed: learners are disengaged because training lacks role-specific relevance, organizations struggle with logistics of training delivery, and there is urgent demand for blended, flexible formats that fit into the reality of modern work.

At the same time, artificial intelligence has emerged as a transformative tool for instructional designers—one that can accelerate our work dramatically but also tempt us toward shortcuts that undermine quality.

And beneath it all, learning science continues to reveal how people actually acquire skills and change behavior, insights that too often remain trapped in academic journals rather than informing everyday design practice.

This book brings these threads together. It offers a framework for designing training that works—training grounded in learning science, delivered through strategic microlearning, focused on performance outcomes, and developed efficiently with AI assistance.

The Four Pillars of Performance-Focused Learning™

This book is built on four interconnected pillars that together form a comprehensive approach to designing training that actually changes behavior.

Learning Science provides the evidence-based foundation. Understanding how people encode, retain, and retrieve information and concepts such as cognitive load, retrieval practice, spaced repetition, and schema building—enables us to design experiences that stick. When you understand why learners forget 70% of new information within 24 hours and what to do about it, your design decisions fundamentally change.

Microlearning applies that science through focused, strategically-timed learning moments that respect cognitive limits and fit into the realities of the modern workplace. But microlearning is not simply "shorter content." It is the smallest meaningful unit of learning that supports a single behavior or objective, designed for precision and delivered at the point of need. When implemented correctly, microlearning becomes a performance tool, not just a delivery format.

Performance Design shifts our focus from content delivery to business outcomes. Rather than beginning with "What content should we cover?" performance design begins with "What organizational results must improve?" and works backward through behavior change to learning design. This approach, anchored in Kirkpatrick's Levels 4, 3, 2 and 1, ensures that every learning intervention targets the critical behaviors that drive organizational results.

AI-Supported Development amplifies our capacity to implement the first three pillars at scale. Artificial intelligence can accelerate content drafting, scenario development, and learning experience creation, but only when wielded by designers (human oversight) who understand learning science and maintain rigorous quality control. AI is a collaborator, not a replacement. It helps us build faster without sacrificing the pedagogical decisions that matter.

These pillars don't stand alone; they reinforce each other. Learning science tells us why microlearning works. Performance design tells us what to build. AI helps us build it efficiently. Together, they transform instructional designers from course builders into performance consultants.

Who This Book Is For

This book is written for instructional designers, learning experience designers, eLearning developers, performance designers, learning architects, educators, trainers, and L&D professionals who create learning experiences and want those experiences to matter.

You may be an instructional designer and eLearning developer for healthcare who has made the shift to performance design, like me. Or you may work in corporate learning and development, higher education, government, nonprofit organizations, or any setting where people need to learn new skills and apply them effectively.

The principles in this book apply across domains. While I draw heavily from my healthcare experience and provide healthcare-specific examples throughout, every strategy, framework, and tool can be adapted to your context. When I describe working with clinical subject matter experts, you can apply those same techniques to working with engineers, attorneys, financial analysts, or any technical experts in your field. When I present a scenario about medication safety, you can translate those design principles to cybersecurity, compliance, customer service, or leadership development.

What unites all readers of this book is a shared frustration: you have seen training that doesn't work. You have built courses that people complete but don't apply. You have measured completion rates and assessment scores while suspecting that the metrics that really matters (e.g., behavior change, performance improvement, organizational results) probably remain unmeasured and possibly unchanged.

You are ready for a different approach.

What You Will Learn

This book is organized as a journey from foundational principles to practical application. I begin by examining the evolution from traditional instructional design to performance design, establishing the mindset shift that underlies everything else. You will learn to think like a performance consultant, not just a course developer.

From there, we explore the science of learning, the cognitive principles that determine whether your training creates lasting change or temporary awareness. You will understand working memory limitations, the power of retrieval practice, why spaced repetition works, and how to apply these principles in practical design decisions.

I then turn to microlearning as the application of learning science in digestible, performance-focused formats. You will learn what microlearning actually is (and what it is not), when to use it, and how to design microlearning that reinforces behavior change. With these foundations in place, we address the practical work of instructional design: understanding your learners beyond demographics, applying backward design and action mapping, creating effective screen designs, developing multimodal learning architectures, and working productively with subject matter experts.

A dedicated chapter explores how to co-design with AI, using artificial intelligence as a collaborative tool that accelerates your work while you maintain control over quality and pedagogical integrity. You will learn prompt engineering techniques, validation processes, and ethical considerations for AI-assisted design.

I address evaluation not as an afterthought but as an integral part of the design process, exploring learning analytics, xAPI implementation, and modern approaches to measuring what actually matters: behavior change and business impact.

Finally, I examine accessibility and universal design, ensuring that the learning experiences you create work for all learners, including those with disabilities. This is not a compliance checkbox but a design philosophy that improves learning for everyone.

Throughout the book, you will find practical examples, case studies from my own work, frameworks you can apply immediately, and tools you can adapt for your context.

A Personal Note

I wrote this book because I believe instructional design matters. When we do our work well, we help nurses provide safer patient care. We help leaders resolve conflicts that were damaging their teams. We help employees master new systems that make their work easier. We help organizations achieve goals that seemed out of reach.

CHAPTER 1

The Evolution of Instructional Design

The profession of instructional design has undergone a significant transformation in recent decades. This transformation is reflected in learning methodologies and technologies and professional titles and role delineations. Yesterday's instructional designers are today's learning experience designers (LXDs), performance designers, instructional architects and learning architects. While these titles reflect the growing demands for workforce skilling; they also share a common purpose, a shift in the demand for learning that is learner-centric, engaging, improve individual performance, that aligns with organizational and business case goals.

Instructional Architects and Instructional Designers

An instructional architect is a professional responsible for designing and structuring learning experiences, much like a building architect creates blueprints for physical structures. These professionals apply learning theories and technology to develop learning experiences that are both effective and engaging. Their work involves identifying learning needs and developing content, activities, and assessments that align with specific goals. The term "learning architect" has emerged in Learning & Development (L&D) as referring to individuals who create comprehensive learning strategies and frameworks grounded in evidence-based learning theories and learning science. Instructional designers who integrate learning theories, frameworks into learning design can also be architects of learning.

The Architectural Analogy: Instructional Designers as Architects of Design

Instructional designers and architects share a common approach: both utilize a structured design process to create products and solutions. This process includes gathering information, conducting analyses, developing concepts, creating prototypes, refining designs, and iterating based on feedback. Both professions balance scientific and artistic elements, employing creative problem-solving to address the specific needs of users.

User-centered design is central to both fields. Architects focus on creating spaces that are functional, visually appealing, and tailored to occupants' needs. Similarly, instructional designers develop learning experiences that are inviting, engaging, and supportive of learners in achieving their educational objectives.

Both architects and instructional designers strive to balance aesthetics and functionality. Architects seek to create beautiful buildings that also meet safety, structural, and operational requirements. Instructional designers aim for visually engaging learning spaces and materials, ensuring that they effectively convey educational content.

Performance Designers: Begin With the End in Mind

Performance Designers begin with Kirkpatrick Level 4 Results, focusing their efforts on achieving tangible organizational outcomes and measurable improvements in behavior and performance. By starting with the end in mind, they reverse-engineer learning experiences to ensure every activity, assessment, and piece of content directly supports the desired business objectives. This approach allows them to identify critical performance gaps and skill needs, strategically selecting interventions that will have the greatest impact. Through close collaboration with stakeholders and a commitment to rigorous evaluation, performance designers create solutions that drive meaningful change, aligning learning initiatives with broader organizational strategies and fostering sustained growth and return on investment.

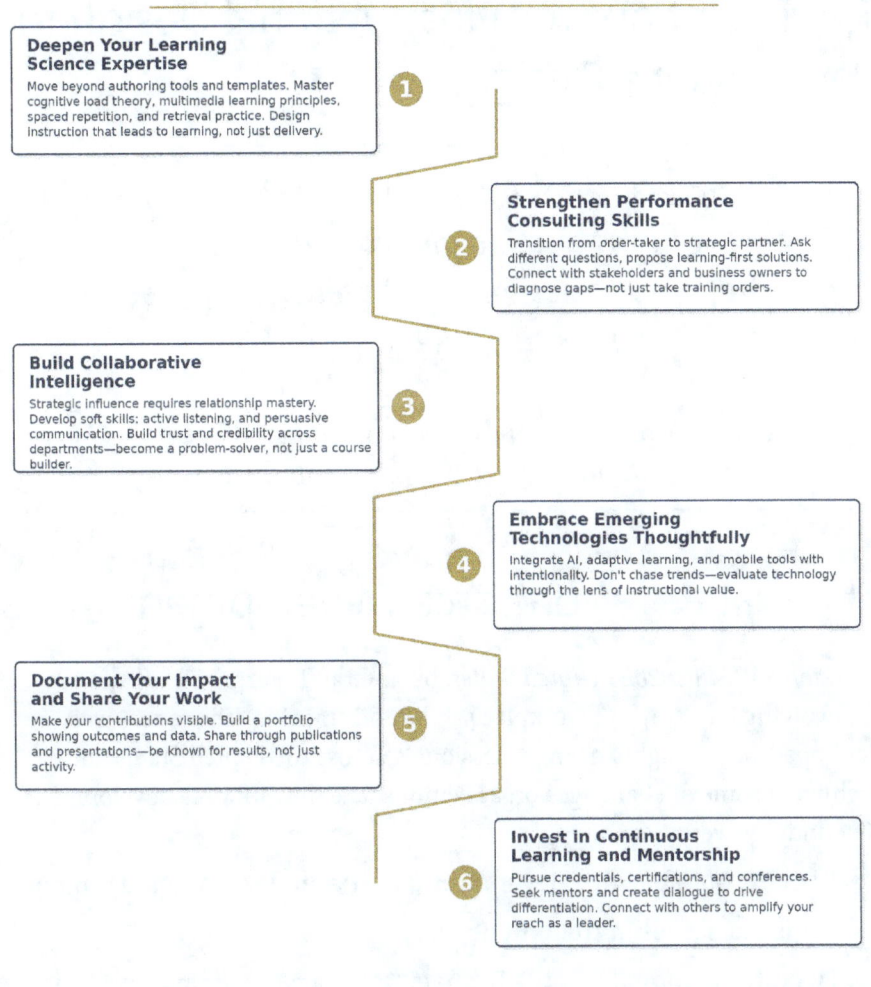

Building Your Roadmap to Strategic Influence

A professional development framework for instructional designers advancing from content delivery to strategic organizational impact

1 **Deepen Your Learning Science Expertise**
Move beyond authoring tools and templates. Master cognitive load theory, multimedia learning principles, spaced repetition, and retrieval practice. Design instruction that leads to learning, not just delivery.

2 **Strengthen Performance Consulting Skills**
Transition from order-taker to strategic partner. Ask different questions, propose learning-first solutions. Connect with stakeholders and business owners to diagnose gaps—not just take training orders.

3 **Build Collaborative Intelligence**
Strategic influence requires relationship mastery. Develop soft skills: active listening, and persuasive communication. Build trust and credibility across departments—become a problem-solver, not just a course builder.

4 **Embrace Emerging Technologies Thoughtfully**
Integrate AI, adaptive learning, and mobile tools with intentionality. Don't chase trends—evaluate technology through the lens of instructional value.

5 **Document Your Impact and Share Your Work**
Make your contributions visible. Build a portfolio showing outcomes and data. Share through publications and presentations—be known for results, not just activity.

6 **Invest in Continuous Learning and Mentorship**
Pursue credentials, certifications, and conferences. Seek mentors and create dialogue to drive differentiation. Connect with others to amplify your reach as a leader.

You are not just a designer of content.
You are an architect of learning experiences that shape performance and culture.

Figure 1.2 Roadmap to Strategic Influence

This roadmap is not a checklist but a compass for growing your influence, refining your practice, and aligning yourself with the strategic needs of your organization or clients. You are not just a designer of content. You are an architect of learning experiences that drives performance outcomes. Join professional organizations such as Association for Talent Development (ATD), Kirkpatrick's Partners, Get Certified in performance design or instructional design, attend L&D conferences, share your knowledge and expertise in a blog, submit proposal to submit at conferences and be a lifelong learner by carefully engaging and obtaining gold standard industry certifications.

The Evolution from Instructional Design to Performance Design

"Success is not measured by the quantity of programs deployed, but by the meticulous design and execution of every learning intervention".

Srikanth Iyengar, CEO-upGrad Enterprise
Workforce Wishlist 2025: United States

The State of Workforce Development

Workforce Wishlist 2025 United States, by upGrad Enterprise explores the evolving landscape of workplace skills and training. The report was developed with insights from professionals across the United States and highlights some of challenges organizations face in workforce development. Key findings were:

- Lack of role-specific relevance as a barrier to learner engagement
- Logistical issues in training delivery
- Need for blended, flexible formats, self-paced learning and live sessions
- Organizations are advised to prioritize leadership, advanced AI/ML, UI/UX design, data science, and cybersecurity training to balance tech and leadership development

This report tells the story of why we must shift to performance design to address workforce development needs. Learners need learning that is relevant, personalized, role-specific and leaders need learning interventions aligned with business goals to drive organizational success. Workforce

Wishlist 2025 emphasizes that L&D (skilling) should not be "relegated to just an HR function but rather a direct driver of profitability and performance goals." Learning interventions must be designed and developed for immediate workplace application with immersive learning experiences and self-paced learning that can be directly applied to workplace tasks, ensuring measurable outcomes.

The Performance Designer: Reframing Learning Through Results

In an era defined by rapid change, digital transformation, shifting expectations, and increasing performance demands, traditional instructional design alone is no longer sufficient to meet today's workforce L&D needs. Organizations need professionals who can diagnose the root causes of performance gaps, design comprehensive solutions that are relevant, role-specific, and connect learning to measurable business goals. This professional is a **performance designer.** This role has emerged as an essential position in L&D and signifies an evolution in instructional design. A performance designer focuses on improving workplace performance. The role has evolved from "What content should be included?" to "What performance outcomes are we aiming to achieve, what are the business case goals, and what practical knowledge and skills must learners develop for proficiency in key tasks? How can real-world context be integrated into the learning experience to ensure its relevance?" How to get stakeholder buy-in? How to measure the return on investment? Adopting this mindset is essential for designing learning and development initiatives that address skill gaps, enhance job performance and organizational goals.

This approach prioritizes identifying the root cause of the performance problem, before content creation. It is important to assess whether the underlying issue is genuinely a learning need or if it reflects deeper concerns, such as fragmented workflows, ineffective technology integration, insufficient system support, or the performance environment (e.g. company culture, lack of accountability, lack of clarity in expectations). As performance designer, identifies which learning interventions are necessary and determines the most effective methods for delivery to participants.

A performance designer does not begin with content; they **begin with results**. Their work is anchored in Kirkpatrick's Levels 4, 3, and 2, they ensure training is not just informational, but transformational. Kirkpatrick offers a Performance Designer Certification course.

Roles and Responsibilities

The performance designer begins by defining the business problem, not the learning problem. They create behavior-driven performance solutions that directly impact organizational success. Their first responsibility is to clarify:

- What organizational results must improve?
- Which business metrics or key performance indicators (KPIs) should training influence?
- What leading indicators show performance is improving?
- What participants need to know (concepts, rules, policies, processes)
- What participants need to do (skills, procedures, decision-making, abilities)
- What they need to believe or feel confident about (mindset, self-efficacy, motivation)
- What participants must commit to (accountability, consistency)

This is not an exhaustive list, rather an introduction of the essential responsibilities. The performance designer is not just an educator or instructional designer, but rather a consultant, analyst, strategist, change agent.

What Makes the Performance Designer Essential Today

A performance designer plays a critical role in 21st century workforce development by:

- Bridging operational and performance data with learning design
- Ensuring training addresses identified performance gaps, not assumptions

- Designing learning interventions that remove barriers to performance
- Partnering with leaders to monitor post-training performance metrics
- Connecting learning outcomes to organizational success
- Creating learning solutions with measurable impact
- Determining critical behaviors to be addressed with training

The Evolution Is Underway

Many instructional designers are already practicing elements of performance design, often without calling it as such. When you map learning objectives to real-world tasks, ask probing questions about workflow challenges, work with subject matter experts (SMEs) to identify skill gaps and author content, design activities and scenarios to simulate workplace decision-making, this is the work of a performance designer, so the evolution has begun.

CHAPTER 2

Learning Science Application: Designing for How People Learn

The evolution from instructional design to performance is already underway. Many learning professionals, whether their title is instructional designer, learning experience designer, learning architects, or performance designer, are expanding their influence beyond content creation designing solutions that enable real behavior change. This shift does not replace instructional design; it builds upon its strongest foundation: **a deep understanding of how people learn.**

Once a performance designer identifies the organizational goals or results that must be improved (Kirkpatrick Level 4), clarifies the on-the-job-behaviors employees must perform (Kirkpatrick Level 3), they must answer a critical question: **How do we design learning in a way that helps people reliably perform those behaviors?** This is the purpose of learning science. Learning science provides evidence-based guidance for how people process information, build skills, develop confidence, and apply new habits. It is the mechanism through which performance design becomes reality. Whether your role is instructional designer or performance designer, mastering learning science enables you to design learning experiences that are engaging and aligned with performance needs.

Instructional designers have long applied learning science principles, often intuitively or implicitly. Performance design makes this application explicit, intentional, and directly connected to the behaviors employees must perform on the job. Whether you are an experienced instructional designer or newly certified performance designer or performance-focused role, mastering learning science is essential. It is the mechanism through which performance change becomes possible.

Learning science tells us how people encode information, how they retain and retrieve information, how they build mental models, how they develop skills through practice, and what supports transfer to real-world performance. It equips designers to move beyond "covering content" to creating learning experiences that reshape thinking, strengthen decision-making, build confidence, and foster new habits.

Designing for how people learn is not an abstract ideal, it is the practical, evidence-based pathway to enabling the critical behaviors identified in performance analysis. In this chapter, we will explore how performance designers and instructional designers apply learning science to answer three essential questions:

- How do we design so people learn effectively?
- What do performance designers and instructional designers actually do when applying learning science?
- How do these practices translate into real, measurable behavior change on the job?

By integrating performance analysis with learning science, instructional and performance designers alike can create learning that is not only formative, but transformative. Learning that turns critical behaviors into consistent habits that drive meaningful results.

The Science of Learning Theory

Science of learning in theory explores the definition of the 'science of learning' and the evidence for it.

The science of learning, grounded in decades of cognitive psychology and neuroscience research, provides a robust foundation for understanding how individuals acquire, retain, and apply knowledge. Far from being a static body of theory, it continually evolves as new studies shed light on the mechanisms underlying memory, attention, and skill development. This evidence base empowers performance designers to craft learning experiences that are not only theoretically sound but also demonstrably effective in supporting behavior change. By leveraging well-established findings—such as the benefits of retrieval practice, the importance of meaningful practice, and the influence of feedback—designers can facilitate deeper understanding and more reliable transfer of learning to the workplace. When carefully applied, the science of learning transforms abstract principles into practical strategies that directly impact how employees think, act, and succeed in real-world environments, seamlessly bridging the gap between instructional intent and measurable outcomes.

Why Learning Science Matters in Performance Design

Identifying the performance gap is only half of the equation. Once we know what learners must do, we must design learning that gives them the cognitive, emotional, and environmental support needed to perform those behaviors confidently and consistently.

To do this, you must draw from the science of learning, for example, concepts such as cognitive load theory (Sweller, 2006), which refers to the amount of information working memory can handle at once, dual coding combining words and visuals to enhance understanding, and spaced repetition. Furthermore, reviewing information at increased intervals over time enhances memory retention and facilitates schema formation, a mental framework that shapes how individuals organize, interpret, and respond to new information and learning. These concepts are not academic footnotes; they are the backbone of effective learning design and essential to performance improvement.

Evidence-Based Practices in Learning Design

Effective learning design is grounded in well-established principles that move beyond theory and provide the framework for successful instructional practices. When creating learning experiences, every interaction, activity, and visual element should be intentionally chosen to serve a distinct cognitive purpose, ensuring that learners benefit from thoughtful design.

Applying Cognitive Principles in Instruction. Introducing new concepts by pairing concise textual explanations with relevant diagrams leverages dual coding, allowing learners to absorb information more effectively. Additionally, planning review activities to occur over several days utilizes spaced retrieval, fostering improved memory retention and helping learners to recall information in the long term. Consistently applying these cognitive strategies leads to learning experiences that are both engaging and firmly rooted in evidence-based methods that enhance comprehension and retention.

Today's learners often face distractions, information overload, and limited support. The performance designer's role is to create clarity, minimize unnecessary complexity, and facilitate the transfer of knowledge to practical situations. Employing research-backed strategies is what distinguishes effective instructional design from basic content delivery.

Stakeholder Collaboration: Building the Right Relationships. Successful performance design is rarely achieved in isolation. Collaboration with subject matter experts, project sponsors, learning leaders, and learners themselves is essential for producing high-quality and usable learning solutions. The ability to cultivate these relationships directly influences the final outcome.

Stakeholder collaboration extends beyond traditional project management. It involves developing a mutual understanding and ensuring expectations are aligned. Instructional designers must translate learning objectives into terms relevant to the organization, clearly communicate design decisions, and effectively manage feedback cycles with professionalism and empathy.

In certain situations, it is necessary to educate partners about the fundamentals of performance design. While subject matter experts possess deep knowledge in their domains, they may not be familiar with effective learning principles. The performance designer or instructional designer must help transform expertise into impactful instruction, requiring active listening, diplomacy, and a careful balance between content accuracy and instructional integrity.

By strengthening your abilities in performance analysis, deepening your understanding of the science of learning, and refining your stakeholder communication skills, you position yourself as more than just a designer of courses. You become a trusted partner dedicated to advancing learning and improving performance.

Driving Performance Outcomes

Instructional design is not merely a creative exercise or a support function. It is a discipline with the power to influence real outcomes in business performance, clinical safety, regulatory compliance, and professional growth. Whether you are an instructional designer or a performance designer, you are accountable not only for learning engagement but also for how well the learning translates into action. The true value of your work becomes clear when it produces measurable results that matter to the organization.

Over the past 25 years, I have witnessed how evidence-based design can close performance gaps, reduce errors, and elevate team capability. These experiences have shaped my belief that design must be both strategic and measurable. Let me share a few real examples that illustrate what happens when learning is done well.

Case Example 1: Enhancing Patient Safety through Scenario-Based Learning

Scenario-based learning (SBL) has shown great promise in enhancing patient safety in the healthcare industry. The effect of SBL on nursing students' core competencies was examined in a study published in *BMC Medical Education* (Alharbi et al., 2024). The results showed that students who took part in SBL significantly improved their clinical skills, communication, self-confidence, and teamwork, which are critical for patient safety.

Similarly, a study by McDade (2023), published in the *Journal of Nursing Education,* demonstrated how successful case-based patient scenario learning exercises are in nursing education. According to the study's findings, these methods improve nursing students' clinical reasoning, assessment abilities, and medication knowledge, all of which lead to safer patient care.

These studies underscore the critical role of instructional design in healthcare education. By implementing scenario-based methodologies, instructional designers can foster environments that not only engage learners but also equip them with the skills necessary to reduce clinical errors and enhance patient outcomes.

Case Example 2: Solving the Learner Engagement Challenge through Microlearning

Microlearning has become a powerful tool for improving learner engagement in health professions education courses and eLearning. Breaking down long lectures and complex topics into short, focused, interactive lessons help reduce cognitive overload, and enhance learner engagement and knowledge retention.

I deployed micro-learning modules in an online course using **Synthesia. io**, an AI-powered video-generation tool to transform lengthy passive lectures into multiple short sessions focused on specific topics and learning objectives, each including interactive case studies, decision points, and reflection activities.

The lectures and activities were mobile ready, allowing busy healthcare professionals to engage with the content on their devices and absorb the material during each microlearning moment. Learner analytics revealed an 86% increase in completed lecture video views and a 90% increase in weekly participation.

Another example from the same course is the use of the 7taps platform to deliver personalized microlearning modules to graduate learners. As learners completed course activities and assessments, I identified skills gaps and created adaptive learning modules, deploying short, outcomes-based lessons to support their development. These brief modules, no longer than 4 minutes, offered adaptive and personalized learning tailored to each learner's performance improvement needs. Content was delivered through video-based lessons, brief role-play simulations, case studies (see figure 2.1) infographics, and quizzes aligned with focused learning objectives. Learner analytics revealed increased engagement and improved posttest performance as a result of integrating microlearning that supported critical thinking and decision making, ultimately leading to better learner outcomes (7taps, n.d.).

Case Study

A conflict is brewing at Sunrise Valley Regional Hospital, where operational changes caused tension between the board and independent medical staff.

Autonomy vs. Sustainability

Physicians feel their clinical autonomy is threatened, while the board prioritizes financial sustainability, resulting in a no-confidence vote against the board chair.

CSO Conflict Strategy

As Chief Strategy Officer (CSO), you have been tasked by the CEO to de-escalate the conflict, rebuild trust, and align organizational goals.

    ← →

Assess the Situation

You must now:

1. Evaluate the situation from an organizational leadership perspective
2. Assess how governance structures and communication breakdowns contributed to the conflict
3. Develop a conflict engagement and resolution strategy that promotes transparency, inclusion and mutual accountability

What is the primary goal of for resolving the conflict?

○ To prioritize financial sustainability over clinical autonomy

◉ To de-escalate the conflict, rebuild trust, and align organizational goals

○ To enforce operational changes without consulting the medical staff

⊕ Add option

Comment (optional)

The primary goal is to de-escalate the conflict, rebuild trust, and align

Figure 2.1 Conflict Resolution Microlesson

Research Spotlight: Retrieval Practice vs. Concept Mapping

The Study: Karpicke, J.D. & Blunt, J. R (2011). Retrieval practice produces more learning than elaborative studying with concept mapping. *Science* (6018), 772-775.

What They Did: College students learned from educational science texts using either concept mapping (creating diagrams while viewing the material) or retrieval practice (setting the text aside and recalling as much as possible from memory).

Findings:
- Retrieval practice produced significantly better performance on a test one week later
- The advantage held even for questions requiring inference and comprehension, not just factual recall
- Students in the concept mapping group were overconfident about how much they had learned

Why this Matters: This study, published in one of the world's most prestigious scientific journals, demonstrates that the act of retrieving information from memory is more powerful than elaborate study techniques, even highly regarded ones like concept mapping. The key isn't how elaborately you process information while viewing it; it's whether you practice reconstructing that information from memory.

The Takeaway for Instructional/Performance Designers: Build retrieval opportunities into your learning experiences. Knowledge checks, practice questions, recall activities, and scenario-based assessments aren't just evaluations tools, they're LEARNING tools. Every time you ask learners to pull information from memory, you're strengthening their ability to access and apply that knowledge when they need it.

From Learning to Performance

Learning science is the bridge between **learning** and **doing**. The use cases presented in this chapter demonstrate how performance design and instructional design utilizing a microlearning delivery approach can directly affect business metrics. By delivering focused, accessible training, organizations can foster continuous learning and drive measurable improvements in performance. When designers understand how people learn, retain, and apply knowledge, they create solutions that genuinely change behavior. Learning science is not optional, it is the foundation of effective performance design.

Grounding instructional design decisions in the principles of learning science ensures that every educational intervention is not only engaging but also strategically aligned with how individuals acquire, retain, and apply knowledge in authentic settings. By integrating evidence-based strategies such as adaptive scenarios, microlearning, and contextualized practice, designers can close the gap between theoretical understanding and practical performance, ultimately empowering learners to succeed amid the complexities and unpredictability of real-world environments.

CHAPTER 3

Understanding Your Learners and Performance

Several years ago, a large teaching hospital in the United States launched an eLearning initiative aimed at reducing medication errors among newly graduated nurses. The module, developed by a third-party vendor, was polished and packed with information. It featured interactive quizzes, clinical scenarios, and animated demonstrations of proper drug administration protocols. The instructional design team followed a familiar path: Extract content from policy manuals, meet with clinical educators, and map the learning objectives to organizational standards. The hospital rolled out the training to all new hires with high expectations (Cook & Artino, 2016).

Six months later, the internal quality team noticed that medication errors had not declined—in fact, they had slightly increased. A cross-functional team of nurse educators, instructional designers, and quality assurance officers launched an in-depth review following implementation. Their findings were sobering, the training had done an excellent job of explaining procedures, but it had missed the mark on preparing nurses for the unpredictable, high-pressure environment of real-world clinical care.

Insights from Staff: Addressing Real-World Challenges

Interviews and focus groups with the nursing staff revealed some common themes. Many of the nurses reported feeling confident immediately after completing the training but were quickly overwhelmed during their shifts. The eLearning had described what to do but not *how to do it in practice*, such as dealing with multiple patients, unclear medication orders, or interruptions from colleagues. The learning failed to reflect the cognitive load and environmental stressors that new nurses experienced on the job. There was also little attention given to the varying levels of prior experience and learning styles within the group; for example, some nurses had years of experience in other countries, while others were transitioning directly from undergraduate programs.

Revised Approach: Learner-Centered Curriculum and Results

The training was revised. Instead of a one-size-fits-all module, the instructional design team created a learner-centered curriculum based on a comprehensive needs assessment, which included direct observation, structured interviews, and input from frontline staff. The revised version incorporated decision-making under pressure, branching scenarios that reflected real hospital dynamics, and opportunities for reflection and peer feedback. The new module was paired with on-the-floor mentorship. Within 3 months, medication errors dropped by nearly 18%, and nursing staff reported feeling more confident and better supported in their roles.

Lessons Learned: Contextual and Learner-Specific Design

This case illustrates the truth that every experienced instructional designer comes to understand: Learning is not content delivery. It's context aware, learner specific, and deeply tied to performance environments. Instructional strategies must begin with the people we're designing for, not the material we're eager to teach.

Beyond Demographics: Getting to the Root of Performance

Many instructional designers stop at surface-level data when trying to understand their audience. Age, job title, education level, these are easy to collect and often required by stakeholders. However, they rarely tell you what you really need to know. To design training that actually helps people do their jobs better, you must go deeper.

That means understanding the daily realities your learners face. What pressures are they under? What systems do they navigate? What interrupts their workflow, complicates their decisions, or increases the risk of mistakes? These aren't abstract questions. They're directly tied to whether the training you build will be useful, or irrelevant.

An effective *audience analysis* reveals more than who your learners are. It digs into what they do, how they do it, and what stands in their way. This means shadowing them on the job when possible, asking open-ended questions, and listening carefully to what they say and what they don't. It means observing the constraints of their environment: the noise, the pace, the technology, the culture. Understanding the learners, including demographics, technological skills, learning preferences, and existing knowledge are essential to designing effective learning experiences to improve performance.

You also need to understand how learning fits (or doesn't fit) into their routines. Do they have time to focus? Are they constantly interrupted? Are they expected to learn during a lunch break or at the end of a 12-hour shift? You can design the most elegant training in the world, but if it doesn't respect the learner's reality, it won't stick.

Another key factor is motivation. What drives your learners? Are they looking to build confidence, reduce stress, gain autonomy, or meet compliance requirements? Are they skeptical about training because of past experiences? You won't get these answers from a survey but from talking to people, building trust, and taking their input seriously.

When you take the time to understand your audience on this level, your design decisions change. You stop leading with what content needs to be covered and start asking, "What does this person actually need to do?" That shift, away from information dumps and toward performance support, can make the difference between training that checks a box and the one that changes practice.

Gathering Real Intelligence: Getting to Know Your Learners

Effective instructional design starts with a simple but often overlooked truth: You can't fix what you don't understand. If your goal is to improve real-world performance, then you need to uncover what's actually happening in the workplace, what's working, what's not, and why. This isn't guesswork. It requires deliberate, systematic methods for gathering insight. And while every context is different, there are core approaches that apply across settings.

Performance Observations

There's no substitute for being where the work happens. Watching people in action gives you a kind of insight you can't get from meetings or data alone. You begin to notice patterns, the way a technician bypasses a screen prompt to save time, how a nurse double-checks a medication label because she doesn't trust the electronic record, or the way team members signal silently to avoid alerting a patient. These aren't things they'd necessarily describe in a survey. but they're real, and they affect how work gets done.

Observation should be focused and intentional. You're not just watching for the sake of watching. You're looking for decision points, barriers, delays, workarounds, confusion, and communication breakdowns. Take detailed notes. Ask quiet clarifying questions. Try to document not just what happens, but why it happens that way. Sometimes it's due to policy, but more often it's shaped by culture, habit, or frustration.

Importantly, this isn't about finding fault with the people doing the work. It's about understanding the reality they operate in and designing solutions that fit.

Listen to the Right People: Stakeholder Interviews

Next, talk to the people who understand the bigger picture. This means frontline staff, yes, but also supervisors, department leaders, compliance officers, and anyone else whose success depends on how well others perform. Their perspectives are often siloed, but together they form a more complete understanding of the learning and performance gaps at play.

A good stakeholder interview is part journalism, part investigation. Don't just ask what content they want covered. Ask what keeps them up at night. What mistakes do they see repeatedly? Where do people struggle once the training ends? What metrics are slipping? What are the downstream consequences when tasks aren't done correctly?

You're trying to connect behavior with outcomes. That's how you move from vague learning objectives to clear performance goals. You also want to get a sense of the organizational landscape: Are there competing priorities? Are there political sensitivities? Who's resistant to change, and who's already on board?

Use these questions to map out the pressures your learners are under—and the expectations they're trying to meet. Often, you'll find a disconnect between what leadership believes and what's happening on the ground. That gap is where smart instructional design can do its best work.

Use the Data: Workplace Analytics and Performance Metrics

While observation and interviews give you the qualitative picture, analytics help you back it up with numbers. If your organization collects performance data and most do in some form, this is the time to dig in. Look at completion rates, error reports, compliance scores, productivity dashboards, call logs, time-to-proficiency stats, incident tracking systems, whatever's available. These aren't just numbers; they're patterns of behavior over time.

What tasks are consistently delayed or done incorrectly? Where do users abandon systems or ignore alerts? Which departments outperform others on key metrics, and why? If possible, pair these analytics with training records. You might find that people who skipped a particular module are more likely to make certain errors, or that new hires coming from a specific program hit competence faster. Use this information to triangulate your findings from observations and interviews.

A note of caution: Don't let the data drive your entire analysis. Numbers can be misleading without context. For example, a spike in medication errors might reflect a change in documentation practices rather than actual mistakes. Always validate what the data seems to show by talking to people and observing the workflow.

Learner Personas

We've established the importance of understanding your audience. Who are you creating the learning experience for, what are the unique characteristics of your audience? Are they adult learners, nurses, physicians, IT staff, etc.? How do they engage with the content, desktop, mobile devices? Are they digital natives? Knowing this helps you tailor the learning experiences to meet the needs of your learners. This is where learner personas can be a powerful tool for creating learning experiences tailored to meet the needs of your audience. So, what are learner personas? Learner personas are fictional profile characters of your target audience. The personas represent typical behaviors, motivations, challenges, and learning preferences, helping instructional designers tailor learning materials.

Pro Tip: Use learner personas to anticipate accessibility needs and integrate inclusive design thinking into storyboarding, prototyping, and developing eLearning projects.

Understanding Generational Differences

Today's workforce is multigenerational, so a one-size-fits-all approach to learning does not meet the diverse needs of learners. Understanding the learning preferences, technological behaviors, and motivations that drive baby boomers, Gen X, Millennials, and Gen Z is essential but often overlooked when designing learning experiences. This insight allows instructional designers to create learner-centric designs that truly meet the needs of their audience. There's nothing worse than spending hours, weeks, or even months designing a high-tech module for a low-tech audience. If you have access to generational data, consider tailoring your learning approach accordingly. If your audience analysis instrument does not include age range, consider adding it. Identifying the generational makeup of your learners can help you design more inclusive and effective learning experiences. This approach ensures that learning solutions are relevant and accessible, bridging the gap between what learners need and what the organization requires. By drawing on generational insights and current data, you can craft profiles that highlight not just demographic differences, but also workplace expectations, technology comfort levels, and engagement styles.

Pulling It All Together

Once you've gathered insight from the floor, the people, and the numbers, your job is to synthesize. What are the consistent themes? Where do learner needs and organizational goals intersect or clash? Where is clear confusion, bottlenecked performance, or a mismatch between expectations and resources?

This step takes time, and you'll be tempted to rush it. Don't. What you uncover here will guide every decision you make going forward. It will shape your objectives, content, delivery methods, and even how you measure success. Sloppy analysis on the front end guarantees weak outcomes on the back.

If there's one thing to remember, it's this: Training doesn't exist in a vacuum. It lives inside systems, roles, routines, and expectations. You can't build effective learning unless you understand those forces. And that understanding doesn't come from your desk. It comes from showing up, asking questions, and really listening to the people who do the work.

CHAPTER 4

Designing in the Real World: What Culture, Tech, and Compliance Mean for Your Course

If you've ever built a learning solution that made perfect sense on paper but crashed into reality the moment it hit the organization, you're not alone. Instructional design doesn't happen in a vacuum. It unfolds inside real systems, with real constraints. And no matter how well you understand your learners, if you ignore the broader environment they work in, your design will fall flat.

There are three forces; organizational culture, technology infrastructure, and regulatory requirements, that quietly shape everything you build. You can't control them, but you can learn to work with them.

Culture: The Water Everyone's Swimming In

Culture isn't just about values printed on posters in the break room. It's how people really behave when no one's watching. It's whether staff speak up when they see a problem. It's whether managers back new initiatives or quietly sabotage them. It's whether training is seen as an opportunity or another hoop to jump through.

Every organization has its own way of getting things done. Some are top-down and risk-averse; others are fast-moving and experimental. In some places, learning is seen as a career booster; in others, it's just another checkbox. These differences matter.

Say you're designing a new onboarding experience for surgical techs. In a high-accountability, team-oriented culture, you might build in simulation labs, mentorship rounds, and real-time coaching. In a more hierarchical setting, where roles are rigid and senior staff resist change, you might need to introduce content gradually, involve department heads early, and find a champion with influence to advocate for the new approach.

Ignore culture, and your program becomes "that thing corporate rolled out." Work with it, and you have a shot at real impact.

Technology: What You Have vs. What You Wish You Had

No matter how creative your ideas are, they have to run on the tech the organization actually uses. This includes learning management systems (LMS), content authoring tools, mobile access, bandwidth limitations, and user devices.

In theory, you might want to create branching scenarios, embedded video demos, or interactive peer feedback loops. In reality, the LMS may not support those features, or learners may be using outdated browsers in shared workstations. Maybe there's no single sign-on, or mobile access is restricted for security reasons. These are real issues, not excuses.

Rather than designing around what you wish you had, get familiar with what's actually in place. Learn the system's limits and its strengths. Sometimes, a simple tool used well beats a flashy tool used badly.

It also helps to develop strong relationships with IT and system admins. These folks can tell you what's possible, what's coming, and what's never going to fly. When you're designing for scale, these conversations are essential.

And don't forget usability. Just because something technically works doesn't mean it works for your learners. If a training module takes too long to load or doesn't remember where someone left off, it's going to frustrate people and erode trust. Tech is part of the learning experience. Treat it like one of your design variables, not an afterthought.

Compliance and Regulation: The Non-Negotiables

In fields such as healthcare, finance, aviation, and manufacturing, regulatory requirements aren't suggestions. They're mandatory. And they directly affect what needs to be taught, how it's tracked, and how often it's repeated.

When designing annual compliance training for a hospital, you must cover Occupational Safety and Health Administration (OSHA) standards, HIPAA regulations, Joint Commission mandates, and internal policies, while ensuring the material remains accessible and engaging for learners.

Too often, compliance training turns into a content dump, with every department insisting their material is "nonnegotiable." But learners aren't regulatory experts— they're professionals trying to do their jobs. Your role is to interpret the requirements, clarify the intent, and design experiences that make the content usable.

This means translating legal or technical language into real-world applications. It means balancing depth with clarity. It might also mean pushing back when the volume of content makes the training ineffective. Yes, you need to meet the letter of the law. But you also need to meet the spirit of learning: relevance, clarity, and retention.

Another important part of working within compliance-heavy environments is documentation. You may need to build in tracking, timestamping, version control, and automated reporting. These needs should be considered from the start, not at the end.

In short, designing effective learning means designing within reality. Culture shapes what people are ready for. Technology determines what's possible. Regulations dictate what must be done. Your job is to hold all three in view and still build something that helps people learn, perform, and grow.

From Insights to Action: Turning Analysis into Design That Works

Gathering insights about your learners is only useful if you do something with them. This is the part where too many projects fall short. Teams spend weeks collecting data from focus groups, workflow observations, interviews and then hand them off to designers with no clear roadmap. What happens next is usually a mix of guesswork, compromise, and too many review meetings.

To avoid this situation, you need a systematic way to translate learner analysis into actual design decisions. Not just content topics, but decisions about structure, pacing, practice, feedback, and measurement. What follows are three practical frameworks that help bridge that gap from raw data to instructional strategy, keeping performance at the center of the process.

1. The "Know-Feel-Do" Framework

Start by organizing your insights into three simple categories:

- Know: What do learners need to understand or remember?
- Feel: What attitudes, beliefs, or emotions are helping or hurting performance?
- Do: What specific tasks or behaviors need to change?

Let's say your analysis shows that nurses are skipping medication reconciliation at discharge because they don't see the downstream impact on patient safety (*feel*), they're not confident in the process (*know*), and the workflow is rushed and inconsistent (*do*). That tells you your course needs more than instructions, it needs a shift in mindset and practical rehearsal.

This framework keeps you grounded. It's not about what stakeholders *want* in the course, it's about what learners need to do their jobs better.

2. Environment–Task–Barrier Mapping

This model is especially helpful in performance-driven environments. You map out

- Environment: Where and when the task is performed?
- Task: What the learner needs to do?
- Barriers: What's getting in the way?

For example, let's say technicians in a lab are frequently mislabeling specimens. Your analysis shows that the task happens during shift changes, when documentation systems are slow to load and staff are multitasking. The barrier isn't just lack of knowledge, it's environmental pressure.

This mapping helps you prioritize design features. Maybe it means creating a 2-minute refresher module that fits into daily huddles. Maybe it's a printable visual guide near the workstation. Maybe it's not a course at all, but a system change.

Not every gap requires training. This framework helps you make that call early.

3. Learning-to-Performance Alignment Table

Insight from Learner Analysis	Learning Need	Learning Strategy	Performance Outcome
Junior sales staff lack confidence in objection handling.	Build confidence and provide practice.	Branching scenario with customer responses and feedback	Staff engage more confidently with hesitant clients.

Table 4.1 Learning-to-Performance Alignment Table

It seems simple but putting things in a table like this forces clarity. If you can't trace a learning activity back to a real performance need, it probably doesn't belong. This format also makes your decisions easier to explain to stakeholders who want to know why you've chosen one approach over another.

Designing for impact isn't about adding more content. It's about choosing the *right* content, at the *right* depth, delivered in a way that fits the learner's world. A strong analysis gives you the raw material. These frameworks help you shape it into something real, something that moves the needle on performance.

When you can do that consistently, you stop being a content builder and you become a design partner. And that's where the real value lies.

CHAPTER 5

Backward Design and Action Mapping for Performance

Several years ago, I was brought in to consult for a mid-sized financial services company struggling with compliance training. The internal audit team had flagged repeated violations in areas employees had already been trained on. The courses were mandatory and the completion rates were high, yet the behavior on the floor showed no measurable improvement. Something wasn't working.

The company's original compliance program was built around annual slide-based modules that covered every policy update in exhaustive detail. It was what you'd expect, bulleted legal jargon, passive narration, and a quiz at the end that employees could take (and retake) until they passed. The focus was on content delivery and documentation, not performance. And that was the root of the problem.

Rather than starting with the slide deck, I started with the audit reports. I met with the compliance officers, team leads, and even a few employees who had failed to follow procedure. The pattern was obvious: Employees were not misinformed, they were overwhelmed. The procedures were complex, varied by department, and required real-time decisions. No amount of policy text could prepare someone for that.

So, we threw out the existing course structure and started from scratch, using a backward design approach. First, we clarified the actual behaviors we wanted to see on the job. Not "understand policy X," but "handle client data in accordance with procedure Y during real-time calls." Once the performance goals were defined, we mapped backward from those outcomes to identify what people needed to do, not just know. This is known as *backward design,* a learner-centric instructional development process that begins with the end in mind. The desired learning outcomes and competencies, rather than starting with content or activities. This framework, developed by Wiggins and McTighe (2004), provides a systematic approach to curriculum development that naturally aligns with competency-based education.

This shift in thinking led us to an entirely different kind of learning solution. We built interactive, scenario-based modules that mirrored the most common compliance challenges reps faced during their day. Instead of reading about a rule, learners practiced applying it in a simulated client interaction. The assessment wasn't a multiple-choice quiz but a branching scenario that showed whether the learner could make the right call in context.

Within a quarter, the compliance incidents dropped by over 40% in the target departments. And when we reviewed the feedback, employees didn't just say the course was more engaging. They said it helped them understand why certain procedures mattered and how to apply them under pressure.

This kind of outcome is exactly what backward design is meant to achieve. It puts the spotlight where it belongs, not on content coverage, but on performance. By starting with the end in mind, you are no longer just delivering training. You are solving a business problem. And that is the role of a learning architect or performance designer.

From Objectives to Outcomes: Using Action Mapping and Understanding by Design

If you have ever sat through a course packed with definitions, policies, and procedures only to leave unsure of what you were actually supposed to do, you already understand the problem Cathy Moore set out to solve with Action Mapping. Her approach cuts through content overload and brings the focus back to behavior, what learners need to accomplish in the real world. When combined with the broader framework of Understanding by Design (Dávila Rubio, 2017), the result is a process that not only simplifies learning design but sharpens its impact.

Action Mapping begins with a deceptively simple yet essential question: What do people need to do on the job? To dive deeper and begin to uncover what's needed to improve performance, ask an even more powerful follow-up question: What tasks are they not doing, or not doing well, that are affecting performance? This shifts the role of instructional design from simply delivering information or "content dumping" to enabling action on the job. Instead of focusing only on what learners need to know, it zeros in on what they need to do. The goal is to identify the specific tasks and behaviors that aren't being performed well and that affect job performance (see Table 5.1). Once the critical workplace behavior is identified, the next question to ask is, What's getting in the way of the task or behavior being performed consistently and accurately? This question helps uncover the root cause of the issue whether it's a lack of knowledge, skills, motivation, tools, or something in the environment. That's where the instructional design work begins—not with a slide deck, but by identifying a performance barrier and designing learning experiences that yield results.

Let's say your organization wants its customer service reps to handle billing disputes more effectively. A traditional training might open with a policy review and escalate through definitions and background. Action Mapping skips all that. Instead, you start by identifying the exact behavior, resolving billing disputes while maintaining customer satisfaction, and then map backward. What decisions do the rep need to make? What mistakes are most common? What environment or tools will they be using? What skills or judgment calls trip them up?

	Knowledge Gap	Employees don't know what to do or why it matters.
☐	Skills Gap	Employees have not had enough hands-on experience or practice or constructive feedback to become competent in performing the task.
☐	Workflow or Time Constraints	Competing priorities and/or unclear processes make it difficult to follow standard operating procedures (SOP).
☐	Unclear Expectations	Performance expectations are not clearly explained, documented, or reinforced.
☐	Motivation	Employees don't see the value or feel confident in their performance.
☐	Environmental or System Constraints	Lack of tools needed to perform tasks efficiently, poor system design, inconsistent tech support affecting performance.

Table 5.1 Common Barriers Affecting Workplace Performance

Understanding by Design (2004) complements this by providing a broader structure for curriculum development. Where Action Mapping excels at zooming in on performance problems, UbD brings a strategic, systems-level view. It pushes you to identify your desired results upfront, determine what evidence will prove learners can perform, and then plan learning experiences accordingly. These are called the "Three Stages of Backward Design":

1. **Identify Desired Results: What should learners be able to do or apply in the real world?**
2. **Determine Acceptable Evidence: How will you know they can actually do it?**
3. **Plan Learning Experiences and Instruction: What experiences will build toward that outcome?**

Together, Action Mapping and Understanding by Design provide a powerful one-two punch: Action Mapping focuses the content on what's truly needed for performance, while Understanding by Design ensures alignment between goals, assessments, and learning activities. The combination is time-saving, fluff-free, and results in the training that the learners do not merely complete but enjoy.

Designing this way does take more upfront effort. It requires stakeholder interviews, access to job data, and a willingness to push back when someone says, "Just teach them everything." But the return is worth it. You reduce cognitive overload, increase transfer of learning, and support actual behavior change.

The next time you're asked to "build a training on X," pause and ask: What problem are we really trying to solve? The answers to that question when clearly mapped out and approached through backward design will form the foundation of a course that actually works.

> **Pro Tip:** Strategic planning is essential to course development especially with corporate eLearning projects. It is important to identify success measures for any L&D or training project. Ask key stakeholders about the business goals and success measures of the training. This is essential for ensuring that your instructional design strategy aligns with business goals and success metrics. It's important to know what a successful L&D or training project looks like in the eyes of the stakeholders.

Bridging the Gap: From Performance Needs to Real-World Practice

Training only makes sense when it addresses a specific performance gap. If there is no gap, there is no problem, and if there is no problem, then there is no reason to build a course. That is the route that so many good-intended learning teams take: reacting to content requests instead of performance needs. Before you open a storyboard and begin writing down learning objectives, you must be clear on what learners are not doing, what the business requires learners to do in its place, and what may be getting in the way.

Start with performance data. Look at productivity reports, audit results, quality reviews, or customer feedback. Identify the gaps. What are the measurable behaviors that are falling short? Are nurses failing to follow a hand hygiene protocol correctly? Are new hires making frequent documentation errors? Is your sales team closing deals slower than the industry average? These gaps are often buried in operational data. Your job is to surface them and ask the right questions.

Then, define the steps the learners must make to reduce the gap. That is where performance mapping comes in, ask subject matter experts or colleagues doing the job well and analyze the job into observable actions that can be trained. Be specific. "Improve communication" is not an action; "Use the SBAR framework to report patient status" is. "Be more efficient" is vague; "Complete intake documentation in under 10 minutes without errors" is measurable.

Now that you know what the learner needs to do, not just know, you can start building the bridge. Design activities that simulate real work. If your goal is to improve clinical handoff reports, build a scenario where learners listen to a rushed patient handoff and identify missing or incorrect information. If your goal is faster claim processing in an insurance setting, create a workflow simulation with distractions, incomplete files, and realistic decision points.

This is where many courses fall short. They describe the job, but they do not allow learners to practice the skills needed to perform well on the job. Experience is the best learning source for adult learners. They must be challenged, tested, and given feedback under environments that closely resemble those that will be met at on the floor, in the field, or at their desks. And they must be allowed to fail safely, as it is when the consequences are perceived to be real, yet the stakes are not that learning is impacted.

Targeted or deliberate practice is not a few knowledge checks or quizzes integrated throughout the course followed by an assessment at the end of a module. It is a decision-making activity based on an actual scenario, aligned to a real job outcome, and followed by meaningful feedback. It is intentional, repetitive, focused, and structured learning designed to improve specific performance. You are not only asking, "Did they get the answer right?" You are asking, "Would they know what to do on Monday morning?"

When you design this way, your training becomes a performance tool, not a presentation. Learners engage with it differently. They recognize that it is built for them, not just about them. And most importantly, after completion of the learning experience, they leave being better prepared to do the work.

Measuring What Matters: Assessing Behavior, Not Just Knowledge

If your course ends with a multiple-choice quiz or test, you are not measuring performance, you are measuring recall. And while knowledge is an essential ingredient in behavior change, it is only the beginning. Instructional designers committed to real impact must go beyond asking what learners remember and begin asking what learners do differently after training. This is where true learning assessment begins: with behavior.

One of the most reliable ways to assess behavior is through *scenario-based evaluation.* You do not test definitions or facts, but you pose situations to learners that most of them will experience in the workplace and require them to make some decisions. Ambiguity, time pressure, or tension provide the best situations, as they are simulated to real life. You are looking for patterns in how learners respond: Do they prioritize safety? Do they escalate appropriately? Do they apply policy with discretion?

To illustrate, in a course on safety in the workplace, you would not say something like, What are the actions in the emergency plan? Rather, you would display a plan of the building, discuss a given type of hazard (e.g., chemical spill or electrical fire), and ask what the learner would do first. The answer they give you indicates what their judgment is like, not only their memory.

The other good strategy would be the in-situ observation, which entails the performance being observed in the real setting. This may include following an insurance agent or nurse during a shift, listening to customer service calls to see whether the tone is right and whether the call is finally answered, or even a sales rep who is making a pitch to a customer. The goal is not to police or criticize. It is to gather evidence of whether the learner is actually applying what they were taught.

For this to work, you need clearly defined performance criteria. What does "successful" look like? Can you see it? Can someone else? Your criteria should be visible, quantifiable, and reflective to what you aim to learn. You also require good raters managers, team leaders, and preceptors who understand what to survey and the manner of providing constructive feedback. Observational data is meaningless unless there is regularity, and then it is anecdotal and hence difficult to take action on. In some organizations, performance dashboards and analytics can serve as a powerful supplement to human observation. If you are training a support team to reduce call handling time without sacrificing quality, post-training performance data can tell you whether the learning worked. If you are teaching a surgical team new safety protocols, compliance audits can provide the evidence.

Triangulation is key. No single method is perfect, but when scenario responses, supervisor observations, and real-world performance metrics all point in the same direction, you know you are on solid ground. You are no longer relying on a score. You are telling a story, one where behavior has changed, performance has improved, and learning has left the classroom.

Evaluating Real Change: Behavior Over Recall

Most training programs still lean heavily on what is easy to measure, such as quiz scores, end of module tests, or course completions. But if you are trying to change what people do at work, that is not enough. *Knowing the right answer and applying it in real life workplace situation are two different things.* Knowing the process is one thing, but do you have the skills or competence to apply what you have learned effectively each time?

One of the more effective ways to measure practical application is through scenario-based assessments. These are not knowledge checks that ask for definitions or steps from memory. Instead, they present situations that feel familiar to the learner, things they might actually encounter on the job. The way they respond tells you whether they understand the concept well enough to act on it under pressure.

Let's say you are building training for a sales team. Rather than asking them to list product features, you could give them a conversation with a hesitant client and ask how they would handle objections. Or in healthcare, you might present a scenario where a nurse must decide what to do when a patient shows early signs of deterioration. The goal is to reflect the real decisions people make and see how well they navigate them.

Another useful method is workplace observation. This does not need to be formal. Sometimes, just watching someone carry out a task and taking a few notes gives insight into whether the training worked. In some cases, managers can handle this informally by checking in during team meetings or performance reviews. What matters is seeing the behavior play out in context.

You can also gather data from existing performance systems. If a learning intervention was designed to reduce errors in documentation, pull a few reports from before and after. If the goal was to improve how quickly a technician completes repairs, check the service logs. These numbers often tell you more than a final quiz ever could.

Whatever method you use, the aim is the same: to understand whether the learning sticks and shows up when it counts. You are not looking for perfect answers. You are looking for habits, decisions, and actions that align with the job.

This is the shift in thinking that separates content delivery from real instructional design. You are not just teaching, you are shaping what happens after the lesson ends.

Building with the End in Mind: A Practical Design Tool

When developing any kind of training, whether it is a short course or a multimodule program, it is easy to get pulled into content lists and stakeholder requests. Everyone has something they want included. Those pieces do not matter though, as long as they connect back to some distinctive performance objective. That is why a backward design approach is vital. It aids you in being focused on the actual thing that matters according to what the learner is supposed to do differently on the job. In this section you, will be provided with a basic template which you can work on. It does not need to be complicated. It should just be thought of as a working draft you revisit as the course crystallizes.

Step 1: Define the Real-World Goal

Start with this question: What should the learner be able to do by the end? Not just what they need to "know" but what they need to do. Use plain, clear action verbs. For example: "Respond appropriately to a patient's medication reaction" or "Log compliance issues following company protocol." If it sounds like something someone would actually say in a workplace, you are on the right track.

Step 2: Determine how you will assess their ability

Now ask yourself: What proof will I have that the learner can perform this skill or behavior? The answer should connect to the real world, not just a quiz. You might use a role-play, a case scenario, a task demo, or a checklist that a supervisor can use on the job. Think about the setting, will this be a classroom, a virtual simulation, or something they do on the floor? Build your assessment to match the context.

Step 3: Outline How They Will Reach Their Goal

Last comes the learning itself. Based on the skill and the assessment, choose the right mix of activities. What do they need to practice? What support do they need; visuals, demonstrations, feedback? Keep only what moves the learner closer to the final goal. If something does not serve that purpose, consider cutting it. That space is better used for meaningful application.

Backward design is not only useful to instructional designers, but also excellent in bringing subject matter experts and managers on the same page. Use it to make expectations clear, to simplify the content, to move the priorities to results and not only to delivery.

CHAPTER 6

Microlearning for Performance

In the previous chapter, we examined how backward design and action mapping serve as practical tools for driving performance improvements. These approaches emphasize starting with the end goal in mind and aligning every part of L&D to clear, actionable objectives that reflect real-world workplace needs.

Building on those foundational concepts, this chapter introduces microlearning as one of the four pillars of this book. Microlearning offers a focused and flexible method for delivering targeted learning experiences that support performance in modern work environments. By understanding microlearning in the context of backward design, readers will see how both strategies work together to create relevant, impactful training that meets the evolving demands of learners and organizations.

As the workforce training demands continue to evolve and modern learners balance competing priorities and less time for learning in the workplace, *microlearning* has emerged as one of the most effective ways to deliver learning that respects times constraints while still driving performance needs. Microlearning has emerged not as a trend or a shortcut, but rather, a strategic design approach grounded in how people learn, remember, and apply new skills in real-world environments.

If you believe microlearning is just about making content shorter and completing a learning event in 3–5 minutes, then like me, you fell for the industry's biggest misconception about microlearning. So, let's explore, *what is microlearning, really?*

What Microlearning Really Is (and Isn't)

Microlearning is the smallest meaningful unit of learning that supports a single behavior or objective. According to Kapp and Defelice (2019), microlearning is a short, focused learning experience that is not time-limited (pp. 29–30). It is not merely chunking or segmenting content into shorter lessons. It is accessible, and designed for immediate application.

What microlearning is NOT:

- Not defined by duration
- Not a shortened course
- Not a replacement for deeper learning
- Not easier to design

When implemented effectively, microlearning serves as a precision tool for closing targeted knowledge or skill gaps, enabling learners to access just what they need, exactly when they need it. Rather than attempting to condense comprehensive courses into bite-sized segments, microlearning is intentionally crafted to address single, actionable objectives; delivering value in moments that matter most. Its power lies in flexibility. **Microlearning modules can be deployed as stand-alone resources, embedded within larger learning modules, or integrated into workflows for performance support.** This approach ensures that learning is not only relevant and accessible, but also seamlessly fits the realities of modern work life, setting the stage for an ecosystem where learning continuously supports performance.

Why Microlearning Works (The Learning Science)

Microlearning aligns with how the brain learns:

- Reduces cognitive load
- Supports spaced repetition
- Encourages retrieval practice
- Helps build schemas
- Uses dual coding
- Supports habit formation

The Science Behind Why Microlearning Works

Microlearning isn't simply a trend born from shrinking attention spans, it's an instructional approach deeply aligned with how the human brain naturally acquires, processes, and retains information. To understand why microlearning is so effective, we need to explore the cognitive science principles that underpin it.

Working Memory and Cognitive Load

Think of your brain's working memory as a small desk where all your active thinking happens. This desk can only hold about four to seven items at once, and it can only process information for roughly 10 to 20 seconds before things start falling off the edges. When we overwhelm this limited workspace, cognitive overload occurs and learning breaks down. Information gets lost before it can be meaningfully processed.

Traditional lengthy training sessions often pile too much content onto this mental desk at once. Microlearning, by contrast, delivers information in small, focused chunks that respect these cognitive limits.

In healthcare: Consider teaching nurses about a new infusion pump. A 90-minute training covering every function, alarm, and troubleshooting procedure creates cognitive overload, too many features competing for limited mental space. A microlearning approach might instead offer a five-minute module on basic setup, followed later by separate modules on programming secondary infusions, responding to occlusion alarms, and documenting in the EHR. Each module addresses one task the nurse can immediately practice.

In any workplace: Imagine onboarding a new employee to your project management software. Rather than a two-hour walkthrough of every feature, microlearning might start with a three-minute video on creating their first task, then a separate module the next day on setting deadlines and dependencies. The learner masters each function before moving to the next.

Spaced Repetition: The Power of Strategic Timing

In 1885, German psychologist Hermann Ebbinghaus discovered something troubling: we forget approximately 70% of new information within 24 hours if we don't revisit it. He called this the "forgetting curve." Different interpretations of his work have the percentage fluctuating from 60% to 80%; however, Ebbinghaus also discovered the antidote, each time we review information at strategically spaced intervals, the forgetting curve flattens. The memory becomes more durable.

Microlearning naturally supports this principle of spaced repetition. Rather than cramming all content into a single marathon session, microlearning spreads exposure across days or weeks.

In healthcare: A hospital rolling out new sepsis screening protocols might introduce the initial screening criteria on day one, send a brief case-based scenario on day three asking staff to identify sepsis indicators, provide a quick refresher on escalation procedures on day seven, and deliver a final competency check at day fourteen. Each touchpoint reinforces and extends the previous learning, building durable knowledge that's available during a real clinical emergency.

In any workplace: An instructional designer teaching managers about giving effective feedback might introduce the SBI model (Situation-Behavior-Impact) on Monday, send a brief practice scenario on Wednesday where managers identify the components in a sample conversation, and follow up the next week with a reflection prompt asking them to describe a real feedback conversation they've had. The spacing transforms a forgettable one-time workshop into lasting behavioral change.

Retrieval Practice: Learning by Remembering

Here's a counterintuitive truth about learning: the act of pulling information out of your memory (retrieval practice) strengthens that memory far more than putting information in (Karpicke & Blunt 2011).

When you struggle slightly to recall something, that moment of effort before the answer comes to you, you're actually strengthening your neural connections to that knowledge.

In healthcare: Instead of simply reviewing medication administration rights (right patient, right drug, right dose, right route, right time), a microlearning module might present a post-operative scenario and ask the nurse to identify which rights are at risk when the pharmacy delivers a medication with a slightly different name than what's in the chart. The nurse must actively recall the rights and apply them, strengthening both memory and clinical reasoning.

In any workplace: Rather than showing employees a video about cybersecurity best practices, a microlearning module might display a suspicious email and ask learners to identify the red flags before revealing the answers. That moment of mental effort, scanning for misspelled domains, urgent language, unexpected attachments, builds the pattern recognition they'll need when a real phishing attempt arrives.

Schema Building: Creating Mental Frameworks

Your brain doesn't store knowledge as isolated facts floating in a void. Instead, it organizes information into interconnected frameworks called *schemas*, mental structures that help you make sense of new information by connecting it to what you already know.

In healthcare: Consider how an experienced nurse approaches a patient with sudden shortness of breath. She doesn't process symptoms in isolation. Her mental schema for "respiratory distress" immediately activates connected concepts: oxygen saturation, breath sounds, patient positioning, potential causes ranging from pulmonary embolism to anxiety, and appropriate interventions for each. This schema was built gradually, through repeated exposure to related concepts and clinical experiences that her brain wove together over time.

A microlearning curriculum for new nurses might build this schema deliberately starting with a module on normal respiratory assessment findings, then abnormal findings, then common respiratory conditions, then prioritization of interventions. Each module adds another layer to the mental framework, with explicit connections to previous content.

In any workplace: Think about how a skilled project manager instantly recognizes the warning signs of scope creep. Her schema for "project risk" connects budget discussions, stakeholder requests, timeline pressures, and team capacity into an integrated mental model. A microlearning series might build this schema for new project managers by first establishing what scope means, then how scope changes occur, then early warning indicators, then response strategies, each module referencing and building upon the previous concepts.

Dual Coding: Two Channels Are Better Than One

"People learn better from words and graphics together rather than words alone," the multimedia principle (Clark & Mayer , 2016). Your brain processes verbal information (words, whether spoken or written) and visual information (images, diagrams, animations) through separate cognitive channels. When you present information through both channels simultaneously this principle is called dual coding (Clark & Mayer, 2023). You essentially give the brain two opportunities to encode and store that knowledge. For example, watching an educational video.

In healthcare: A module on wound staging becomes more memorable when the verbal description of a Stage 3 pressure injury ("full-thickness skin loss with visible fat, but no exposed bone, tendon, or muscle") appears alongside clinical photographs showing exactly what that looks like. When a nurse later assesses an actual wound, she can recall both the verbal criteria and the visual reference, improving accuracy.

In any workplace: Compliance training on workplace harassment becomes more impactful when the verbal definition of hostile work environment is paired with a brief animated scenario showing the subtle escalation of inappropriate comments. Learners encode both the policy language and the visual representation of how these situations unfold, making them better equipped to recognize real instances.

Habit Formation: Making Learning Automatic

Another piece of the microlearning puzzle involves understanding how habits form. Habits are behaviors that become automatic through repeated practice in consistent contexts. They follow a neurological loop: a cue triggers a routine, which delivers a reward, reinforcing the pattern.

The brief, accessible nature of microlearning makes it ideal for building learning habits. When a five-minute module becomes part of someone's routine, triggered by a consistent cue and rewarded by a sense of completion, learning becomes embedded in daily life rather than relegated to occasional training events.

In healthcare: A nursing unit might establish a brief "safety moment" at the start of each shift, where staff complete a two-minute microlearning module on their mobile devices while waiting for handoff report. The shift start becomes the cue, the quick module is the routine, and the visible completion checkmark (plus the dopamine hit of finishing a task) serves as the reward. Within weeks, this learning habit requires no willpower, simply what the team does.

In any workplace: An instructional designer might build a learning habit by completing one professional development microlesson each morning while their coffee brews. The brewing coffee becomes the cue, the brief lesson is the routine, and the combination of caffeine and new knowledge creates the reward. Over a year, these small daily investments compound into significant expertise.

Microlearning Formats That Work

Microlearning offers distinct formats chosen based on learning goals, delivery platforms, and learner preferences. Use Table 6.1 to select microlearning strategies for your course design.

Microlearning Type	Learning Need
Video Nuggets	Short videos (2–5 mins) focusing on a specific skill or task. Ideal for demos or storytelling. Example: A nurse demonstrating proper handwashing technique.
Infographics	Visual summaries of key info. Great for step-by-step guides. Example: The 5 rights of medication administration.
Interactive Scenarios	Learners make decisions and see consequences. Useful for soft skills. Example: Handling a difficult patient interaction.
Quizzes and Polls	Quick knowledge checks or opinion polls. Reinforces learning. Example: Choosing next steps in stroke protocol.
Flashcards	Cards for quick recall of definitions or terms. Example: Medical abbreviations or dosage conversions.
Podcasts/ Audio Clips	Short audio clips (5–7 mins). Great for on-the-go listening. Example: A doctor's reflection on ethical decision-making.
Job Aids/ Checklists	Printable/downloadable guides for performance support. Example: Pre-op checklist for surgical prep.
Text Messages/ Mobile Alerts	Bite-sized mobile tips/reminders. Example: Daily medication safety tips.
Simulations or Games	Interactive tools for risk-free practice. Example: A code blue response simulation.
Social Microlearning	Learner discussions via forums or chat. Encourages peer learning. Example: A prompt on leadership tactics in a crisis.
Slide Decks or Animated Explainers	5–7 slide decks or animations teaching one concept. Example: Animated steps to interpret a patient chart.

Table 6.1 Microlearning Strategies

Making Microlearning Stick: Content Atomization, Skill Building, and Reinforcement That Works

Effective microlearning is not just about chunking long content into smaller chunks. That's not a strategy, it's just editing. What really makes microlearning work is a methodical approach that starts with how people actually perform tasks in the real world.

My approach is to start by identifying a specific performance goal. I ask, what does the learner need to do, not just know? What are they not doing now and why? Once I've got the answer, I map out the actions required to perform that task correctly. This is where content atomization begins.

What Is Content Atomization?

Content atomization is a key strategy for effective microlearning. It is the process of breaking down complex information, concepts, or learning materials into their smallest, most manageable pieces known as "atoms" of content. Rather than presenting a learner with long, dense modules or overwhelming them with too much information at once, atomization aims to create bite-sized segments, each focused on a single topic, objective, or skill. We use content atomization because it

- **Reduces Cognitive Overload:** By presenting information in smaller, focused units, learners can absorb and retain knowledge more easily.

- **Increases Flexibility:** Learners can access just the information they need, exactly when they need it, allowing for just-in-time learning and efficient performance support.

- **Supports Progressive Learning:** Each atom builds on prior knowledge, enabling learners to master foundational skills before moving on to more complex material.

- **Enhances Learner Engagement:** Short, targeted content is easier to fit into a busy schedule, making it more likely that learners will complete modules and revisit them as needed.

The atomization process typically involves

- Analyzing learning objectives or tasks
- Identifying the smallest meaningful units of content
- Structuring these units logically, so each one stands alone but can also fit into a larger learning progression
- Designing each atom for clarity, focus, and rapid consumption—often in under 10 minutes.

Examples of Content Atoms

- A 3-minute video showing how to perform one step of a procedure (e.g., handwashing)
- A single-page infographic illustrating a core concept
- A brief quiz on one learning objective

Content atomization underpins microlearning and just-in-time training by reducing material to essentials and delivering it in brief, accessible formats, enabling learners to quickly acquire skills and knowledge as needed.

By leveraging these principles, microlearning delivers immediate value to learners by making content digestible, memorable, and actionable. It not only facilitates quick access to essential knowledge but also reinforces learning through repeated, targeted exposures and real-world application. As we move forward, it is important to understand how microlearning can be strategically embedded at different touchpoints to maximize its impact on performance and development.

Microlearning Integration

Performance Ecosystem: In a performance ecosystem, microlearning becomes a dynamic resource, supporting learners before, during, and after formal training, and providing just-in-time tools within the workflow. This integration ensures that learning is always available in context, bridging gaps precisely when they arise and reinforcing new skills as they are needed.

- **Before training**: (Prime & Prepare), short explainer videos as prerequisite concepts primers, a quick list of glossary terms, animated overview of processes or anatomy & physiology, pre-assessment questionnaires; reduces cognitive overload during training by assessing that foundational knowledge is accessible

- **During training**: (Reinforce & Retrieve) micro-scenarios, knowledge checks, reflection questions; leverages retrieval practice to deepen learning and identify gaps

- **After training**: (Sustain & Space) reinforcement, reminders, certification preps, spaced retrieval; transforms short-term training gains into long-term knowledge gains.

- **In the Flow of Work**: (Support & Perform) job aids, decision support tools, troubleshooting aids, policy refreshers, quick reference guides, bridge the gap between learning and doing

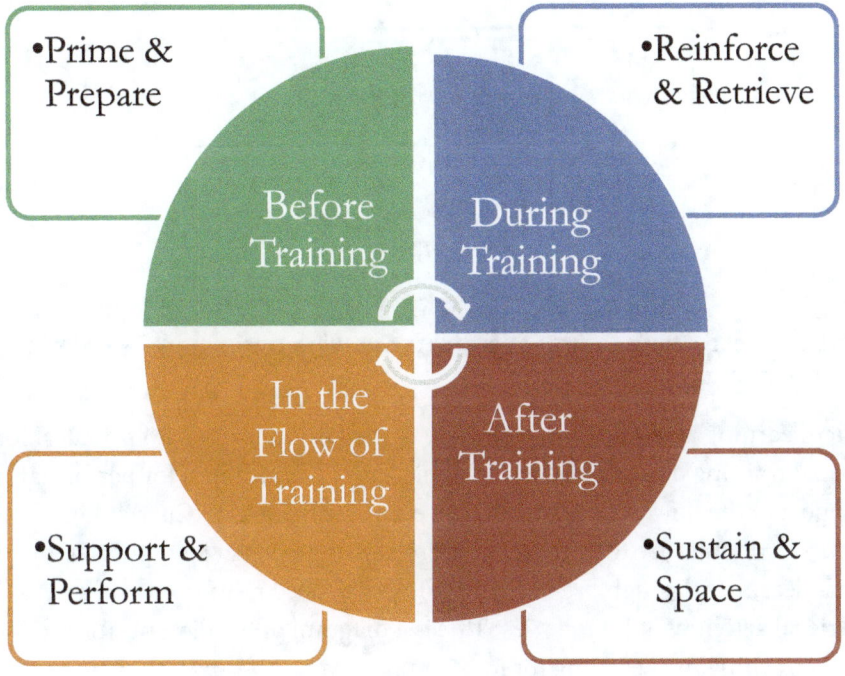

Figure 6.1 Microlearning Performance Ecosystem

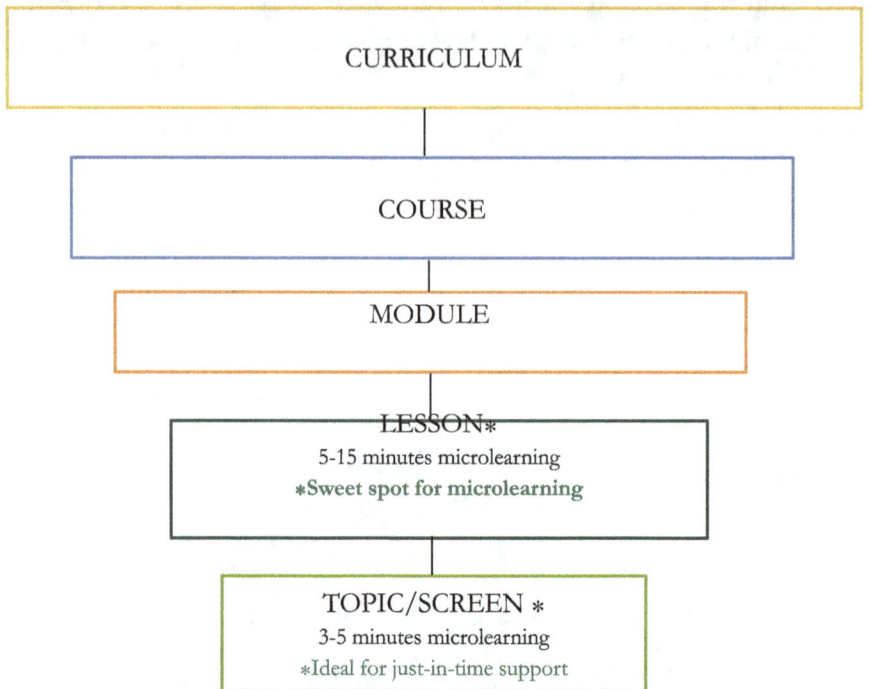

Figure 6.2 eLearning Course Hierarchy: Showing optimal placement for microlearning

Microlearning assets are most effective at the Lesson level (5–15 minutes) for formal training delivery and at the Topic level (2–5 minutes) for performance support in the flow of work. Higher levels of the hierarchy (Curriculum, Course, Module) are too broad for microlearning but can be supported by microlearning through pre-training primers, spaced reinforcement, and retrieval activities at boundaries. This is a diagram of how I've positioned microlearning in eLearning for maximum impact.

By embedding microlearning strategically throughout the performance ecosystem, organizations can ensure that learning interventions are targeted, timely, and aligned with real-world needs. Whether delivered as quick primers to set the stage, as interactive scenarios to reinforce skills during formal training, or as job aids and decision tools within daily workflows, microlearning becomes an integral part of supporting continuous development. This holistic integration empowers learners to access relevant resources exactly when challenges arise, fostering a culture where learning is not a discrete event but an ongoing process that enhances performance at every stage. As the next step, designing microlearning for performance requires a focused workflow that ties each module to specific goals and measurable outcomes, ensuring that every learning touchpoint contributes to sustained growth and impact.

Designing Microlearning for Performance: A Practical Workflow

Step 1: Identify the Performance Goal

Step 2: Identify behavior that needs improvement

Step 3: Atomize the Content

Step 4: Choose the Right Format

Step 5: Design for Clarity

Step 6: Sequence and Reinforce

Step 7: Review and Test

Step 8: Measure Performance

By following this workflow for designing microlearning, organizations can directly link learning experiences to tangible improvements in performance. After refining and measuring each module, the next logical step is to consider the platforms and tools that best facilitate rapid development and ongoing engagement. For instance, solutions like the 7taps Microlearning Platform enable creators to deliver content in formats such as flashcards, micro-scenarios, and audio insights, all optimized for mobile accessibility and spaced reinforcement. Integrating these tools into the workflow ensures that microlearning remains adaptive and responsive to learners' needs, supporting continuous improvement and providing meaningful analytics to guide future iterations. As microlearning evolves, attention to both format and delivery becomes essential for maximizing retention and fostering real-world application, laying the groundwork for effective, scalable learning solutions.

Microlearning in Practice: 7taps Microlearning Platform for Learning Reinforcement and Retention

In this training, the core curriculum is delivered through a traditional three-module eLearning course. 7taps microlearning platform was used to deploy spaced-repetition microlearning campaigns. Rather than functioning as a content library, platforms like 7taps are typically used to design short, targeted learning sequences that support behavior change, reinforcement, and decision-making in the flow of work.

Two examples from my microlearning sequence on human trafficking: Each element is designed to prompt a specific action; noticing a signal, making a judgment, or recalling the correct response under pressure; rather than simply consuming information.

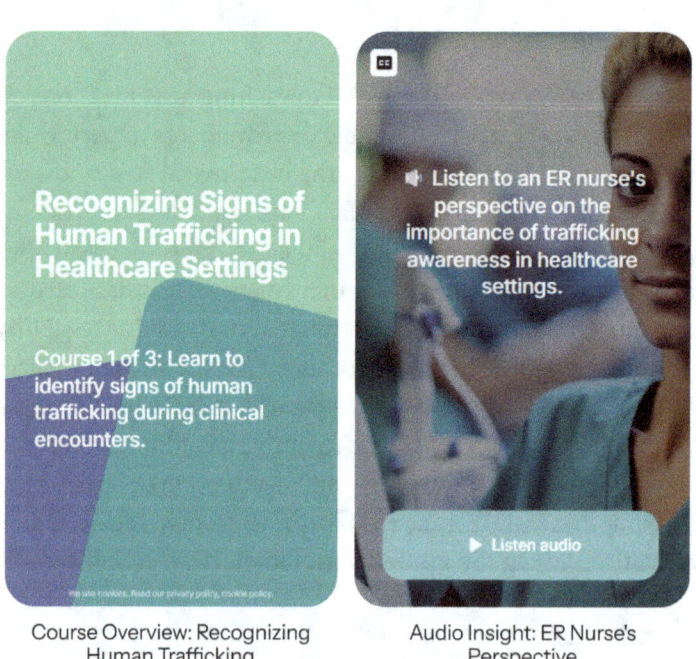

Microlearning in Action: Overview and Audio Insight

Course Overview: Recognizing Human Trafficking

Audio Insight: ER Nurse's Perspective

Figure 6.3 Microlearning Overview and Audio Insight

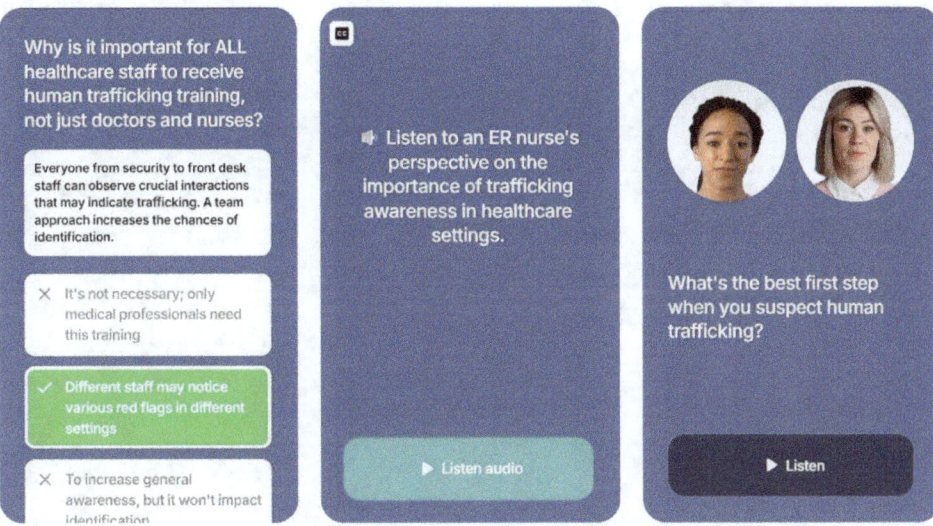

Figure 6.4 Micro-Scenario and Reinforcement Cards

Conclusion: Microlearning Is about Performance, Not Just Time

When used strategically, microlearning strengthens performance, boosts retention, and accelerates behavior change. As we've explored in this chapter, microlearning is most effective when it is intentionally aligned with real-world performance, supporting learners before, during, and after training, and bridging the gap between knowing and doing. Nowhere is this alignment more critical than in healthcare and the health professions, where cognitive load is high, errors carry real consequences, and learners must quickly translate knowledge into safe, accurate clinical practice. In the next chapter, we shift our focus to the specialized world of instructional design and designing for performance in medical and nursing education. You'll learn how microlearning, performance design, and learning science principles come together in environments defined by fast-paced decisions, complex procedures, and high-stakes outcomes. Chapter 9 will show you how to design for the realities of healthcare environments, balancing medical complexity, instructional clarity, and learner needs to create educational experiences that truly improve patient care.

CHAPTER 7

Co-Designing with AI for Performance

Connecting AI to the Performance Design Framework

In Chapter 1, we explored the evolution from instructional design to performance design shift from asking "What content should be included?" to "What performance outcomes are we aiming to achieve?" In Chapter 2, we established that learning science is the bridge between learning and doing, grounded in evidence-based principles like cognitive load theory, retrieval practice, spaced repetition, and schema building.

Now we arrive at a critical question: How does artificial intelligence fit into this performance-focused, learning science-grounded approach?

The answer is not that AI replaces our expertise. The answer is that AI, when used strategically, amplifies our capacity to design learning interventions that drive measurable performance outcomes. AI becomes a co-designer—not an author, but a collaborator that accelerates the work while we maintain control over the pedagogical decisions that matter.

This chapter will show you how to integrate AI into your workflow in ways that align with the book's four pillars: learning science, microlearning, performance design, and AI-supported training. You will learn to use AI not as a shortcut, but as a strategic tool for creating training that works.

Why Performance Designers Need AI Literacy

The Workforce Wishlist 2025 report highlighted critical challenges facing today's organizations: lack of role-specific relevance, logistical barriers to training delivery, and the need for blended, flexible formats. These are not content problems, they are design problems. And they are precisely the problems AI can help solve when wielded by a skilled performance designer.

Consider what AI enables:

Rapid Analysis and Synthesis. When a stakeholder hands you 200 pages of policy documents and asks for a 15-minute microlearning module by Friday, AI can help you extract key concepts, identify critical behaviors, and draft initial content structures in hours rather than days.

Scale Without Sacrificing Quality. The Workforce Wishlist emphasized that L&D must be "a direct driver of profitability and performance goals." AI allows you to create role-specific variations, adaptive learning paths, and personalized reinforcement at a scale that was previously impossible.

Alignment with Learning Science. AI can help you apply evidence-based principles systematically, generating spaced retrieval campaigns, creating scenario-based assessments, and structuring content to reduce cognitive load if you know how to prompt it correctly.

But here is the critical distinction: AI does not know your learners. It does not understand your organizational context. It cannot determine which behaviors will drive performance outcomes. This your area of expertise. AI is powerful, but only when directed by a performance designer who understands both the science of learning and the realities of workplace performance.

The Performance Designer's AI Framework

Before opening any AI tool, ground yourself in the performance design process established in Chapter 1. AI fits into your workflow at specific points and knowing where it adds value (and where it does not) is essential.

Where AI Adds Value

Content Generation and Drafting. AI excels at producing first drafts quickly. Use it to generate initial outlines, draft scenario dialogue, create assessment items, image generation, alt text, video generation and rephrase complex information in plain language. Always treat outputs as rough drafts requiring your revision and validation.

Applying Learning Science at Scale. Once you understand principles like retrieval practice and spaced repetition, AI can help you implement them systematically. You can prompt AI to generate spaced retrieval campaigns, create varied practice questions, or structure content to minimize cognitive load.

Creating Variations and Adaptations. Need the same core content adapted for three different roles? AI can help you create role-specific versions efficiently while you ensure each version addresses the correct critical behaviors.

Scenario and Case Study Development. AI is particularly effective at generating realistic workplace scenarios, branching dialogue, and case study snippets. You provide the context and critical decision points; AI helps flesh out the details.

Where AI Falls Short

Performance Analysis. AI cannot conduct stakeholder interviews, observe the workflow challenges, or identify the root causes of performance gaps. This diagnostic work requires human judgment and organizational knowledge.

Determining Critical Behaviors. Kirkpatrick 's framework reminds us that training must target critical on-the-job behaviors (Level 3) that drive organizational goals (Level 4). Don't leave it solely to AI to assess and determine which behaviors matters most, your analysis and collaboration with stakeholders are essential to identifying critical behaviors and determining if training is the answer.

Validating Accuracy. In healthcare, compliance, and other high-stakes domains, AI-generated content must be verified against authoritative sources. AI confidently produces plausible-sounding content that may contain errors. Your subject matter experts and evidence-based sources remain essential.

Understanding Learner Context. AI does not know that your nurses work 12-hour shifts and complete training on mobile devices during brief breaks. It does not know that your organization just went through a merger and morale is low. You bring this contextual intelligence to every design decision. So, when prompting AI it's important to add context.

Integrating AI into the Performance Design Process

Let me walk you through how AI fits into each phase of performance-focused design work.

Phase 1: Define the Performance Problem

This phase happens before you open any AI tool. You must clarify:

- What organizational results must improve? (Kirkpatrick Level 4)
- Which business metrics or KPIs should training influence?
- What on-the-job behaviors must employees perform? (Kirkpatrick Level 3)
- What is the root cause of the current performance gap?

AI alone should not answer these questions. This requires stakeholder conversations, performance data analysis, and observation of the work environment. However, once you have answers, AI can help you articulate them clearly. You might prompt:

"I am designing training for emergency department nurses. The organizational goal is to reduce patient boarding time by 25%. The critical behavior is accurate and timely completion of admission documentation. Help me articulate 3-4 specific, observable behaviors that support this goal."

Notice that you are not asking AI to determine the behaviors, you are asking it to help you refine and articulate behaviors you have already identified through analysis.

Phase 2: Design the Learning Architecture

With critical behaviors identified, you design the learning experience. This is where learning science (Chapter 2) and microlearning strategy converge with AI assistance.

Structuring for Cognitive Load. Chapter 2 established that working memory can hold only 4-7 items at once. AI can help you chunk content appropriately:

"I have the following content on sepsis recognition protocols [paste content]. Break this into 5-7 microlearning modules of approximately 5 minutes each, with each module focused on a single learning objective. Ensure the sequence builds schema progressively."

Building Retrieval Practice. The research by Karpicke and Roediger demonstrated that retrieval practice is one of the most powerful learning strategies available. AI can help you create retrieval opportunities:

"Generate a 30-day spaced retrieval campaign for sepsis recognition training. Include retrieval prompts for Day 1, Day 3, Day 7, Day 14, and Day 30. Each prompt should require learners to recall information from memory before seeing feedback. Vary the format: some open-ended recall, some scenario-based application, some recognition questions."

Designing Scenario-Based Learning. The 5C framework (Context, Challenge, Choices, Consequences, Conclusion) provides cognitive scaffolding for scenario-based learning. AI can help generate scenarios while you ensure they target the critical behaviors:

"Create a branching scenario for nurse managers on conflict resolution. Use the 5C framework. Context: Two department heads in escalating conflict affecting patient care. Challenge: The learner must intervene. Choices: Provide four options aligned with the Thomas-Kilmann conflict modes. Consequences: Show realistic outcomes for each choice. Conclusion: Synthesize key principles and prompt reflection."

Phase 3: Develop Content

This is where AI provides the most obvious efficiency gains—but also where discipline is most important.

Drafting with Intention. Never prompt AI without clear parameters. Compare these two approaches:

Weak prompt: "Write content about hand hygiene."

Strong prompt: You are an instructional designer creating a 3-minute microlearning module for frontline healthcare workers. The learning objective is upon completion of this lesson the learner will be able to: identify the 5 WHO moments for hand hygiene. Write concise body text (under 100 words) that presents the 5 moments in a memorable way. Use plain language appropriate for varied literacy levels. Do not include lengthy introductions, get to the point immediately.

The strong prompt incorporates principles of cognitive load theory focused on concise text, appropriate reading level, removal of extraneous content.

Generating Assessment Items. AI can rapidly generate assessment questions, but you must specify the cognitive level and format:

"Generate 5 scenario-based multiple choice questions assessing application of the 5 moments for hand hygiene. Each question should present a realistic clinical situation and ask learners to identify which moment applies. Include plausible distractors based on common misconceptions. Provide rationales for correct and incorrect answers."

Creating Role-Specific Variations. When the same core content must reach different audiences, AI helps create variations efficiently:

"Adapt the following medication safety content for three audiences: (1) Registered nurses, (2) Pharmacy technicians, (3) Medical assistants. Adjust examples, terminology, and scope of practice references appropriately for each role. Maintain the same core learning objectives."

Phase 4: Validate and Refine

This phase requires human oversight. AI-generated content requires:

Accuracy Review. Cross-reference clinical content against current guidelines (CDC, WHO, professional association standards). Verify policy content against organizational documents. Check regulatory content against authoritative sources.

Subject Matter Expert Review. Engage licensed practitioners to review clinical scenarios, verify terminology, and confirm realistic decision pathways. Their feedback catches errors AI cannot detect.

Alignment Check. Confirm that all content directly supports the critical behaviors identified in Phase 1. Remove anything that does not contribute to performance outcomes, regardless of how well-written it may be.

Learning Science Audit. Apply the cognitive load checklist from earlier chapters. Verify that screens are focused, visuals serve instructional purposes, and retrieval opportunities are present.

Phase 5: Implement and Measure

Deployment and measurement close the performance design loop. AI can assist with creating evaluation instruments:

"Design a Level 3 evaluation survey to assess whether nurses are applying the 5 moments for hand hygiene in practice. Include questions about frequency of application, barriers encountered, and confidence level. Align questions with the critical behaviors identified in training." However, interpreting results and adjusting the training strategy requires human judgment about organizational factors AI cannot discover. Design a Level 1 survey to assess learner reaction to the training. Did they find the learning event engaging and relevant to their job?

Prompt Engineering for Performance Designers

The quality of AI output depends largely on the quality of your prompts. Skilled prompt engineering separates erronous AI experiences from genuinely quality useful collaboration.

The Role-Task-Format Framework

Structure prompts with three components:

Role: Tell the AI what role to adopt. *"You are an experienced instructional designer specializing in healthcare education..."*

Task: Specify exactly what you need.*"Create a 5-minute microlearning script on proper donning and doffing of PPE..."*

Format: Define the output structure. "Format as: (1) Hook/attention grabber, (2) Core content in 3 chunks, (3) Practice opportunity, (4) Summary. Keep total word count under 400."

Prompts Aligned with Learning Science

Here are prompt templates that incorporate the evidence-based principles from Chapter 3:

For Reducing Cognitive Load: "Simplify the following technical content for frontline staff with varied educational backgrounds. Use plain language, short sentences, and concrete examples. Remove jargon unless essential. Target an 8th-grade reading level. [Paste content]"

For Retrieval Practice: "Create 5 retrieval practice questions for [topic]. Questions should require learners to generate answers from memory, not recognize correct options. Include: 2 open-ended recall questions, 2 scenario-based application questions, 1 question asking learners to explain a concept in their own words."

For Spaced Repetition: "Design a 4-week reinforcement campaign for [training topic]. Week 1: Daily 2-minute review activities. Week 2: Every-other-day practice scenarios. Week 3: Twice-weekly application challenges. Week 4: Weekly integration assessments. Each touchpoint should require active recall, not passive review."

For Schema Building: "Organize the following content to build learner understanding progressively. Start with foundational concepts, then add complexity. Explicitly connect new information to previously introduced concepts. Use analogies to link new material to familiar knowledge. [Paste content]"

For Dual Coding: "Suggest visual elements to accompany the following text content. For each major concept, recommend a specific type of visual (diagram, flowchart, photograph, icon) and describe what it should depict. Visuals should add information, not merely decorate. [Paste content]"

Prompts for Microlearning Development

Microlearning requires particular precision in AI prompting because brevity demands clarity:

For Lesson-Level Microlearning (5-15 minutes): "Create a microlearning module on [topic]. Single learning objective only. Structure: 1-minute context setter, 3-minute core instruction, 2-minute practice activity, 1-minute summary. Total content should be consumable in one focused session."

For Topic-Level Performance Support (2-5 minutes): "Create a just-in-time job aid for [task]. Format for mobile viewing. Include: What to do (3-5 steps maximum), common mistakes to avoid, when to escalate. No background theory—assume user needs to perform this task right now."

For Spaced Retrieval Snippets (under 2 minutes): "Create a Day 7 retrieval prompt for [topic]. Present a brief scenario requiring application of [concept]. Ask learner to respond before revealing expert feedback. Keep total interaction under 90 seconds."

Building Trust: Validation and Quality Control

AI-generated content requires systematic validation, especially in healthcare and other high-stakes domains. I use a structured review checklist before approving any AI-generated content:

Content Validation Checklist

Accuracy

- Is the content factually correct?
- Does it align with current guidelines and standards?
- Have I verified claims against authoritative sources?

Alignment

- Does the content directly support identified critical behaviors?
- Does it align with stated learning objectives?
- Have I removed tangential information?

Tone and Voice

- Does the content reflect organizational voice?
- Is the tone appropriate for the audience?
- Have I eliminated AI-typical phrases ("dive into," "it's important to note")?

Learning Science

- Is cognitive load managed appropriately?
- Are retrieval opportunities embedded?
- Does structure support schema building?

Inclusivity

- Are examples and scenarios diverse and representative?
- Have I checked for implicit bias in language or assumptions?
- Are accommodations for accessibility addressed?

When to Involve Subject Matter Experts

Always involve SMEs for:

- Clinical content involving patient care decisions
- Regulatory or compliance content with legal implications
- Technical procedures where errors have safety consequences
- Content representing organizational policy

SME review is not optional in these domains. AI can draft; humans must validate.

Remember, even a strong prompt does not guarantee quality. Every output must be read with a critical eye. I never publish anything from a model without checking sources and confirming the information aligns competencies and learning objectives. I compare key facts against trusted databases, peer-reviewed journals, or institutional resources and SMEs.

AI Tools in the Performance Ecosystem

Different AI tools serve different purposes in performance-focused design. Here is how I categorize them:

Large Language Models (ChatGPT, Claude, Gemini)

Best for: Content drafting, scenario development, prompt-based generation, analysis and synthesis of source documents, creating variations and adaptations.

Workflow integration: Use throughout the design and development phases. Always with human review and revision.

Organizational considerations: Many organizations restrict use of public AI tools due to data privacy concerns. Understand your organization's AI use policy before pasting any proprietary content into these tools.

AI Video Generation (Synthesia, HeyGen, Colossyan)

Best for: Creating presenter-led video content without production crews, rapid updates to compliance and policy training, multilingual content delivery, scaling consistent messaging.

Workflow integration: Use when video format serves learning objectives and traditional production is impractical. Particularly valuable for content requiring frequent updates.

Performance design connection: Video avatars can deliver scenario-based coaching at scale, as demonstrated in the practical application later in this chapter.

AI-Powered Authoring Assistants

Best for: Generating assessment items, creating interactions, suggesting content improvements, accessibility checking.

Workflow integration: These tools embed AI within authoring environments you already use, reducing context-switching.

Adaptive Learning Platforms

Best for: Personalizing content delivery based on learner performance, identifying knowledge gaps, optimizing learning paths.

Workflow integration: These platforms operationalize the spaced repetition and retrieval practice principles from Chapter 6 at scale. They adjust what learners see based on their demonstrated mastery.

Performance design connection: Adaptive systems connect directly to Kirkpatrick Level 2 (learning), providing data on where learners struggle and succeed.

Ethical Responsibilities in AI-Assisted Design

Using AI as a co-designer carries ethical obligations that extend beyond technical accuracy.

Bias Awareness

AI models reflect biases present in their training data. Watch for:

- Scenarios that default to certain demographics or roles
- Examples that assume particular cultural contexts
- Language that excludes or marginalizes groups

Actively prompt for diversity: "Ensure scenarios include diverse names, backgrounds, and contexts. Avoid defaulting to any single demographic."

Transparency

Be transparent about AI use when appropriate. If your organization has disclosure requirements, follow them. If learners ask how content was created, answer honestly.

Data Privacy

Never paste sensitive data into public AI tools:

- Patient information (even de-identified)
- Employee personal data
- Proprietary business information
- Confidential strategic documents

If you need AI assistance with sensitive content, work with your IT and legal teams to identify approved solutions, which may include enterprise AI deployments or private instances.

Intellectual Property

Understand the terms of service for AI tools you use. Some tools claim rights to content generated on their platforms. Others do not. Know what you are agreeing to.

Human Oversight

Ultimately, you are responsible for everything that carries your name or your organization's name. AI is a tool. The judgment, the ethics, and the accountability remain yours.

From Experiment to Integration: A Maturity Model

Organizations and individuals move through stages of AI adoption. Understanding where you are helps you plan appropriate next steps.

Stage 1: Exploration

You are experimenting with AI tools, testing what they can do, and learning their limitations. Focus on low-stakes applications: brainstorming, drafting internal documents, exploring capabilities.

Stage 2: Selective Integration

You have identified specific use cases where AI adds value and have established personal workflows that incorporate AI assistance. You are developing prompt engineering skills and quality control processes.

Stage 3: Systematic Application

AI is embedded in your standard design process. You have templates, checklists, and review protocols. You can articulate where AI helps and where it does not. You are training colleagues on effective practices.

Stage 4: Strategic Optimization

You are measuring the impact of AI-assisted design on efficiency and quality. You are contributing to organizational AI governance. You are pushing boundaries of what AI can support in performance design.

Most readers are in Stages 1 or 2. That is appropriate. Move deliberately, build competence, and expand AI integration as your skills and organizational readiness grow.

Practical Application: AI-Enhanced Leadership Development

The following case study demonstrates how the principles in this chapter come together in practice. This scenario-based coaching approach was introduced earlier in the chapter and illustrates the integration of learning science, performance design, and AI technology.

The Challenge: Scaling Executive Coaching

Healthcare organizations face a leadership development paradox. Soft skills development (e.g., conflict resolution, de-escalation, emotional intelligence) have never been more critical. Yet traditional executive coaching costs $15,000-$50,000 per leader annually. A health system with 100 senior leaders would need $1.5-$5 million per year for individual coaching. This is fundamentally a performance design challenge: How do we develop critical leadership behaviors at scale, with consistency, at manageable cost?

The Solution: AI Avatar Coaching

Using Synthesia.io, I developed scenario-based coaching that delivers evidence-based leadership development through AI-generated video. But the technology is not what makes this work, it's the content aligned with learning outcomes and the instructional design grounded in performance improvement.

A Complete Scenario: Navigating Interdepartmental Conflict

Context (Setting the Stage)

The AI avatar introduces herself as an executive coach and establishes the learner's role as COO of a 450-bed academic medical center. ED throughput has deteriorated 40% over three months. Two department heads are in escalating conflict. Patient safety is at risk.

Notice how this mirrors performance design principles: we begin with an organizational result that must improve (throughput), identify the critical behavior the learner must perform (effective conflict intervention), and create authentic, real-world context.

Challenge (The Presenting Problem)

The avatar describes the heated exchange between department heads. Accusations fly. Body language becomes defensive. The situation has reached a crisis point.

This challenge is designed to create conflict, the learner must engage actively with a realistic dilemma, not passively receive information.

Choices (Decision Points)

The learner chooses from four options, each representing a different conflict management approach from the Thomas-Kilmann framework:

A. Competing/Directive Approach

B. Avoiding Approach

C. Accommodating Approach

D. Collaborative Approach

Each choice is a plausible response. There are no obviously wrong answers, only different approaches with different consequences.

Consequences (Learning Through Outcomes)

Here is where AI avatar coaching demonstrates its power. Rather than simply telling leaders "collaboration is best," the avatar shows what happens with each choice.

If the Learner Chooses the Competing Approach

When the learner selects the Competing or Directive approach, the AI avatar narrates: By using this approach, an individual prioritizes their own concerns over those of others, leveraging whatever power or authority is available to secure their preferred outcome. This win-at-all-cost mentality often results in the other party feeling disregarded or marginalized.

As the situation unfolds, one leader experiences significant frustration and decides to leave the discussion. The immediate outcome is an escalation of underlying tensions between the parties involved. The unresolved conflict festers, and within three weeks, a formal grievance is filed, illustrating the long-term consequences of relying solely on the Competing approach to manage workplace disagreements.

If the learner chooses the Collaborative approach

When the learner selects the Collaborative approach, the AI avatar narrates: You have shift the dynamic. Both leaders recognize shared problems. Together, you develop solutions. Over the next quarter, admission delays decrease 40%.

This is retrieval practice and scenario-based learning at work. Learners experience outcomes, not just information.

Conclusion (Synthesis and Transfer)

The avatar synthesizes key principles and prompts reflection: "Think about a current conflict in your organization. What interests not just positions are at play? How might you reframe a blame-focused conversation into collaborative problem-solving?"

This transfer prompt is essential. Without it, learning stays in the scenario rather than moving to the workplace.

Why This Works: Learning Science in Action

This scenario embeds the learning science principles embedded throughout this book.

Connectivism. The AI avatar functions as a knowledge node learners access at the point of need, consistent with Siemens' connectivism theory.

Scenario-Based Learning. The 5C framework provides cognitive scaffolding. Learners make decisions and experience outcomes in a safe environment.

Social Learning. Per Bandura's social learning theory, the avatar serves as an expert model demonstrating both actions and reasoning.

Retrieval Practice. Each decision point requires learners to retrieve and apply conflict resolution principles, strengthening retention.

Implementation Considerations

Creating effective AI avatar scenarios requires:

- Subject matter expertise in the content domain
- Instructional design knowledge of scenario frameworks
- Scriptwriting skills for authentic dialogue and to fact-check AI
- Assessment design to ensure learning outcomes
- Understanding of adult learning principles

Technology alone does not create effective learning. The instructional design underneath determines whether AI avatars deliver value, tone, quality, realism or just novelty.

Conclusion: AI as Amplifier, Not Replacement

Throughout this book, we have built a framework for designing learning that drives performance. Learning science tells us how people encode, retain, and apply knowledge. Microlearning delivers focused content that respects cognitive limits. Performance design ensures training targets the behaviors that matter. AI-supported development accelerates our work without compromising quality.

AI fits into this framework as an amplifier. It makes good designers more efficient. It helps experienced performance designers scale their expertise. It allows rigorous application of learning science principles across more content than we could create manually.

But AI does not replace the fundamentals. It cannot conduct performance analysis. It cannot determine critical behaviors. It cannot validate accuracy in high-stakes domains. It cannot understand your learners' context.

You remain essential. Your expertise in learning science, your skills in performance analysis, your judgment about what will work in your organizational context, YOU cannot be automated.

Use AI deliberately. Ground every AI interaction in your performance design framework. Validate ruthlessly. Stay in the driver's seat.

And remember, the goal has never been to create training. The goal is to improve performance. AI is one more tool in service of that mission.

Chapter Summary

Key Principles:

1. AI is a co-designer, not an author. It accelerates work while you maintain control over pedagogical decisions.

2. AI fits specific points in the performance design process: content generation, learning science application at scale, creating variations, and scenario development. It does not replace performance analysis, behavior identification, or accuracy validation.

3. Prompt engineering determines AI output quality. Use the Role-Task-Format framework and incorporate learning science principles in your prompts.

4. Validation is mandatory. Use structured checklists, involve SMEs for high-stakes content, and verify against authoritative sources.

5. Ethical responsibilities include bias awareness, transparency, data privacy, and intellectual property considerations.

6. AI-enhanced learning, like AI avatar coaching, works because of instructional design, not despite it. Technology enables instructional design improves effectiveness.

Reflection Questions:

- Where in your current workflow could AI add the most value?

- What learning science principles could you apply more systematically with AI assistance?

- What validation processes would you need to implement before using AI-generated content in your organization?

- How does your organization's AI policy affect what tools and approaches are available to you?

CHAPTER 8

Working with Subject Matter Experts (SMEs)

Working with Subject Matter Experts (SMEs) to improve workplace performance builds on the foundations of AI-assisted instructional design and the application of learning science by emphasizing the collaborative role of SMEs in shaping effective training solutions. By partnering with SMEs, instructional designers can ensure that learning objectives align with actual workplace requirements and that content reflects current practices and standards. This collaboration supports the creation of realistic scenarios, assessments, and simulations that not only reinforce core competencies but also address performance gaps identified during analysis. Integrating SME expertise throughout the design process enhances the relevance and accuracy of training materials, encourages knowledge sharing, and results in tailored learning experiences that drive measurable business outcomes. This approach compliments established best practices like action mapping and scenario-based learning, providing a direct link between theory, technology, and practical workplace improvement.

The Role of the SME in Performance

Subject Matter Experts (SMEs) play a critical role in driving workplace performance by collaborating closely with instructional designers. Their expertise ensures that learning objectives are not only relevant but also grounded in the realities of current workplace practices. By contributing up-to-date knowledge and insights, SMEs help shape training content that aligns with actual job requirements and standards.

SMEs support the development of realistic scenarios, assessments, and simulations that address specific performance gaps identified during analysis. Their involvement throughout the instructional design process enhances the accuracy and relevance of training materials. This collaboration promotes knowledge sharing and results in learning experiences tailored to organizational needs, ultimately supporting measurable business outcomes.

Integrating SME input is essential for reinforcing core competencies and maintaining alignment with business goals. Their guidance complements established best practices such as Action Mapping and scenario-based learning, creating a vital connection between instructional theory, technology, and practical workplace improvement.

Key Considerations for Success

1. Establish Clear Boundaries and Expectations

Subject Matter Experts (SMEs) bring extensive expertise and experience to instructional design projects. However, they may not always be familiar with effective learning strategies and the distinction between comprehensive reference material and focused learning content. It is important to set expectations early in the collaboration to ensure that the training developed meets learners' needs and organizational goals.

- Clarify the Difference Between Reference Material and Learning Content: SMEs should understand that not all information is suitable for inclusion in training materials. Instructional designers must emphasize the value of streamlining content to prioritize what learners need to know to perform successfully in the workplace.

- Emphasize "Less is More" in Educational Design: Focusing on essential information helps learners retain critical knowledge. Designers should discuss with SMEs why concise, targeted content leads to more effective learning outcomes.

- Highlight the Importance of Measurable Learning Objectives: Early conversations should establish that all content included in the training must support specific, measurable objectives. This focus ensures that learning experiences are purposeful and aligned with business needs.

- Outline Time Commitments for Content Development and Review Cycles: Setting clear expectations around time required for content development and multiple review cycles help SMEs plan their involvement. This preparation supports smoother collaboration and ensures that the instructional design process remains on schedule.

2. Respect the Context

Subject Matter Experts may sometimes resist the simplification of content, preferring to present information in its fullest form. It is important to acknowledge and respect this concern, as it stems from their desire to maintain the integrity and depth of their expertise. However, instructional designers should help SMEs understand that effective instructional design focuses on improving the retention of critical information for learners. By streamlining content, training materials become more focused and accessible, ultimately enhancing the learning experience and supporting the achievement of key objectives.

3. Plan for Multiple Review Cycles

To ensure high-quality training materials, it is important to allocate sufficient time for several rounds of review throughout the project timeline. A structured review process allows for thorough examination and refinement of both content and instructional design, ultimately leading to more effective learning experiences.

- Initial Content Review: Begin with a comprehensive review of the raw content provided by SMEs to confirm completeness and relevance.

- Instructional Design Integration: Incorporate the reviewed content into the instructional framework, aligning it with established learning objectives and design standards.

- Content and Context Accuracy Verification: Conduct a detailed check to verify the accuracy of the information and ensure that it is presented within the correct context for learners.

- Final Approval After Design Implementation: Obtain final sign-off from stakeholders and SMEs after all content has been integrated and formatted within the training course.

Essential Tools for SME/Instructional Designer Collaboration

1. Structured Content Templates

Create standardized templates with the guideposts to assist SMEs in providing content needed to create an impactful learning experience that improves performance.

2. Content Gathering Interview Guide

Prepare structured questions that extract usable content:

- "Walk me through what a new nurse needs to know about [topic] in their first week."
- "What's the biggest mistake you see clinicians make with this?"
- "If you could only teach three things about this topic, what would they be?"
- "What would you ask to test if someone really understands this?"

3. Digital Collaboration Tools

- Google Workspace or Confluence: For team collaboration
- Notion or Padlet: For organizing content relationships
- Loom or Camtasia Screen recorders and screen captures: For SMEs to record explanations of complex procedures
- Virtual Meeting Platforms
- Slack and/or Teams

4. File sharing

- **GitHub or GitLab:** For technical content
- **SharePoint:** For document management
- **Dropbox or Box:** For file sharing with external SMEs

5. Content Validation Checklists

Provide SMEs with specific criteria for reviewing content:

- Current best practices
- Standard Operating Procedures
- Regulatory compliance
- Real-world applicability
- Appropriate complexity level

Best Practices for SME Collaboration

1. Begin with the end in mind.

Begin every project by clearly defining:

- Who the learners are (experience level, role, context)
- What behavior change you're trying to achieve
- How success will be measured
- What constraints exist (time, budget, technology)

2. Use the "Rule of Three"

When SMEs want to include extensive detail, guide them using the "Rule of Three":

- What are the three most important concepts?
- What are the three most common scenarios?
- What are the three biggest risks if someone gets this wrong?

3. Create Content in Stages

Break content development into manageable phases:

- **Content outline approval:** Get agreement on scope and structure.
- **Draft content review:** Focus on accuracy and completeness.
- **Instructional design integration:** Review how content fits into learning activities.
- **Final validation:** Confirm the finished product meets training needs.

4. Establish Communication Protocols

Set clear expectations about

- Response timeframes for reviews
- Preferred communication channels
- Meeting schedules and formats
- Decision-making authority
- Escalation procedures for disagreements

Managing Common Challenges

The "Everything Is Critical" SME (content bloat)

Challenge: SME wants to include excessive detail because "it's all important."

Solution: Focus on job-relevant scenarios. Ask. "In what situations would a learner need to know this level of detail?"

The "Perfectionist" SME

Challenge: SME requests endless revisions for minor details.

Solution: Establish review criteria upfront and stick to agreed-upon approval processes

The "Too Busy" SME

Challenge: SME agrees to participate but doesn't respond to requests.

Solution: Break content development into smaller chunks and provide multiple ways to contribute (calls, emails, recorded videos)

The "Conflicting Opinions" Challenge

Challenge: Multiple SMEs disagree on content or approach

Solution: Establish a lead SME with final decision authority, or create content that acknowledges different approaches when appropriate

Measuring Success

Track these metrics to evaluate your SME collaboration process:

- **Content accuracy:** Post-launch error rates and correction requests
- **Development efficiency:** Time from content request to approval
- **SME satisfaction:** Willingness to work on future projects
- **Learner outcomes:** Achievement of learning objectives and behavior change
- **Relevance:** Feedback from learners about real-world applicability

Review and Feedback

To facilitate the review and feedback process for e-learning modules, utilize the built-in review features within the course authoring tool. This allows stakeholders and subject matter experts to provide targeted feedback directly on the course materials, streamlining revisions and ensuring content quality.

For ongoing communication and collaborative feedback among team members, leverage platforms such as Slack or Microsoft Teams. These tools support real-time messaging, discussion threads, and file sharing, which help maintain clear communication throughout the review cycle.

Conclusion: Building Effective SME Partnerships

Achieving successful collaboration with subject matter experts (SMEs) demands a combination of patience, well-defined structure, and mutual respect. Establishing these elements within the partnership paves the way for productive interactions, ensuring that both instructional designers and SMEs are aligned in their goals and expectations.

When this collaborative relationship is cultivated and functions effectively, it leads to the creation of learning experiences that are not only pedagogically sound but also highly relevant to the needs of the learners. The resulting content meets performance objectives and helps bridge the gap between theory and practice.

Ultimately, the partnership between instructional designers and SMEs is a significant relationship, one that warrants ongoing attention, appreciation, and care. Investing in nurturing this collaboration benefits all stakeholders and contributes to meaningful learning outcomes.

CHAPTER 9

Multimodal Learning for Performance

In today's world learning happens anytime, anywhere on desktops, laptops, and mobile devices. The role of the instructional designer has evolved from mere content and screen design to that of an experienced architect of learning. Now more than ever, designing for performance requires a deliberate and systematic approach to selecting and integrating multimodal learning that meets diverse learner needs and aligns with what the learner needs to do with the content to gain the knowledge, skills, and abilities needed to improve performance.

Multimodal learning architecture is guided by the principle that *form follows function*, a concept from architect Louis Sullivan (1886). This means the way something works should shape its design. In instructional design, this translates to focusing on the training's purpose and intended learner outcomes.

Every modality selected for a L&D project must serve a clear instructional purpose aligned directly to performance objectives, grounded in learner's role and responsibilities and real-world context. Whether designing for new nurses transitioning to practice, a leadership development course for healthcare administrators, or compliance training, instructional design decisions must support both *learning* and *doing*.

When I receive content for storyboarding and development, my first step is *diagnostic*. I review the performance outcomes or learning objectives, complexity of the tasks to be learned, and the environment in which the learning will be applied. Then I match the learning modality to the desired behavior change, not the opposite. In my career, too often, I have witnessed organizations invest in the newest technology without considering if it's the right tool for the job. My goal with instructional design and development is to build a learning architecture where each component has a clear function, alignment, and a congruent learner experience. Who exactly are we designing for? And what are the gaps and causes leading to undesired job performance? What's getting in the way? These questions drive everything else. Especially the delivery format.

The Power or "Why This, Not That"

Choosing the right mix of modalities is a strategic process guided by learning outcomes, not a checklist. For basic knowledge transfer, I use short articles, visual guides, or videos. For complex tasks such as clinical decision-making, I design interactive scenarios with feedback. There is no universal formula—I alternate between microunits, live workshops, or blended approaches such as flipped classrooms, always adapting to the goals at hand.

One of the most important decisions you'll make as an instructional designer is how the learning is actually going to happen. Not the content, yet, but the delivery: Does the learning need to be on demand? Are learners joining live sessions with a facilitator? Are they learning on the job? Or is it some combination of all three?

The choice on what delivery format to use is not random. It's series of tradeoffs and questions that are rooted in the learning goals, realities of the workplace, and the habits of the learners.

Imagine you are designing a program for medical assistant. There's foundational knowledge they need to absorb, policies, medical documentation standards, patient interaction protocols, and scope of practice. This content can lead to desired learning outcomes delivered asynchronously. Self-paced modules give learners time to review at their own speed, revisit information, and manage around shift work.

Hands-on clinical competencies? Not the best fit for asynchronous delivery format. It's difficult to teach and assess proper venipuncture or proper placement of EKG leads purely through slide decks and videos. The learner needs practice, and the educator needs to evaluate that proper techniques, clinical guidelines, and patient safety measures are performed by the learner to ensure competency. This requires a synchronous or experiential learning delivery format.

The blended learning approach uses asynchronous tools for background and context, then bring people together (physically or virtually) for application. That way, we don't waste time covering what could've been read in an email. The live time is spent practicing, troubleshooting, and reflecting. For example, live virtual sessions, via Zoom or Teams, are effective for training needed in the affective domain. Simulated environments or role-play activities on patient engagement, and effective communication skills followed by synchronous (in-person) practice in brick-and-mortar simulation lab with guided supervision from educators give learners the opportunity to try, fail, and improve.

Another factor is culture. Some workplaces lean heavily toward real-time communication. Others are more comfortable with independent work. If you design a fully self-paced program for a team that thrives on collaboration and discussion, you're going to miss the mark. The reverse is also true.

Then there's logistics. Do learners have time to attend in-person training? Are learners spread across multiple time zones? Is there enough tech support to run a synchronous course well? These details matter, and they shape your decisions. Start with what learners need to do, figure out the best way to support that learning, and match your delivery method to the goal.

Instructional designers must know and understand what instructional delivery modality to use and when to meet the needs of the organization, the learner and achieve optimal learning outcomes. Synchronous learning is used when real-time interaction adds value. Asynchronous supports autonomy and flexibility. Blended learning makes sense when physical and virtual formats are needed to achieve optimal performance outcomes.

Designing for Continuity Across Modalities

Oneof the most common sources of confusion for me in instructional design is the term *learning modalities*. There are learning modalities (often referred to as learning styles), learning modalities referring to how instruction is structured and delivered (e.g., asynchronous, synchronous, blended learning) and learning modalities that reference the types of learning technologies (e.g., VR, AR simulations), which defines how a learner engages with content within a delivery framework. For the sake of clarity, this book refers to "modalities" as outlined in the Table 10.1 (Note: This table contains only some common examples; it is not a comprehensive list.)

Modality Type	Meaning	Examples
Learning Modalities	Learner-centered preferences for processing information (learning styles)	Visual, auditory, kinesthetic, tactile
	Delivery formats or channels through which instruction is delivered	Synchronous, asynchronous, blended, experiential
Learning Technology Modalities	Tools, environments or strategies used to create types of learning experiences	Simulations, VR, AR, ePortfolios, AI, peer-to-peer learning

Table 9.1 Modalities in Instructional Design

Let's continue. Writing learning materials for multiple formats—such as virtual classrooms, self-paced modules, and in-person simulations—is not as challenging as making the process feel unified. Learners should experience a logical and connected sequence, not random activities. Start by evaluating how each format supports overall performance goals. For example, when training clinicians on a new documentation system, a live virtual session can cover main features and Q&A, while a follow-up module lets learners practice independently.

Learners practice their skills through virtual simulations, lab sessions, or experiential learning, engaging with real-world scenarios and receiving direct feedback. Each stage builds on the previous one, eliminating wasted time and content repetition.

Instructional designers often run into trouble when designing parts separately, leading to inconsistent tone or terminology. To prevent this, align materials early, use consistent vocabulary and examples, and agree on storytelling across formats. Even small wording changes such as calling something a "critical check-in" in one format and a "touchpoint" in another can make the experience feel disjointed.

Pacing is important. For example, you can use the same ER case throughout the training. Learners document the visit in the self-paced section and make decisions about it in the virtual simulation. Reusing familiar details reinforces learning without being repetitive.

It is important to consider how learners will access each part of the program. Determine whether a phone, tablet or electronic health record is required, if sessions will be recorded, and whether transitioning between platforms could affect the experience. These questions should be addressed at the beginning of the planning process rather than after materials have been developed.

Designing across modalities means building a seamless learning journey, not simply adding more content or tools. Learners should transition smoothly from a virtual session to a self-paced module without feeling disjointed—this is effective design.

Exploring Emerging Modalities: VR, AR, Simulations and Peer Learning in the Real World

New modalities appear as learning environments continue to keep changing. It is true that the tools of virtual reality, augmented reality and peer-to-peer learning programs are no longer exotic but are actively being put to work to address concrete instructional issues today. The thing is to understand where they belong in your ecosystem and how to utilize them purposefully.

Virtual Reality

Let's start with virtual reality (VR). There are industries where VR is not a shiny add-on anymore, at least, not in healthcare, manufacturing, and public safety. It is a tool that enables individuals to practice high-stake skills within an environment that can be controlled. Consider a nurse training in an emergency room in a virtual trauma bay or a technician training to build complex machinery without risking damaging real equipment.

Immersion is what makes VR so powerful. When done correctly, it eliminates outside distractions and enables students to give their full attention to the task at hand. However, it must also be linked to results. VR can have a significant effect if the objective is to enhance decision-making in high-pressure environments. The novelty quickly fades if it is only used to impress stakeholders.

Augmented Reality

Augmented reality (AR) differs from VR in that it integrates digital elements into the physical environment rather than creating a fully digital experience. For example, a nurse might use a tablet to access dosage guidelines by pointing it at a medication cart, or a new employee could scan equipment tags for real-time operating instructions. AR is typically implemented during work processes rather than in formal training sessions, serving primarily as a performance support tool. This shift reflects an increasing overlap between learning and work activities.

Simulations

Simulations are one of the most effective instructional experience modalities in learning and development. They provide learners with a safe, controlled simulated environment to practice skills, make decisions, and learn from mistakes before performance is required in real-world settings. In healthcare, simulations are a cornerstone of clinical practice and education. However, simulations are used from training across disciplines from flight simulations, advance manufacturing, firefighting, law enforcement training, leadership development, soft-skills training and conflict resolution.

Simulations take many forms, from low-fidelity branching scenarios to fully immersive high-fidelity virtual reality environments with VR headsets to simulate real-world conditions for learners. The most common types of simulations include

- Decision-making scenarios
- Clinical skills practice
- Simulated systems training

Simulations offer impactful learning that sticks by

- Providing real-time feedback and consequences
- Allowing learning by doing, not passively watching
- Enhancing knowledge retention
- Bridging the gap between theory and practice
- Providing mastery learning design
- Providing a safe environment to learn from mistakes

Simulations are a powerful instructional modality because they facilitate decision-consequences protocols in a realistic environment, helping learners gain the skills and confidence needed for success on the job. Simulations can be integrated into asynchronous, synchronous, or blended learning delivery formats, sequenced with reinforcement strategies such as coaching, microlearning, or reflection exercises.

When designing simulations focus on real performance tasks, use authentic decision points, consequences, and branching feedback loops to align with what learners must do on the job, not just what they need to know. Work with a SME to gain insights on the workplace environment, roles/responsibilities, and workflow, and incorporate this into your design.

Peer-to-Peer Learning

Peer-to-peer learning platforms are valuable tools, as employees often learn from each other as much as they do in formal training. These platforms let staff share tips, answer questions, and guide colleagues through various experiences, whether via an organized community or a quick Slack group. Such knowledge sharing helps close the gap between structured learning and daily work.

The main issue with any modality isn't access, but alignment. Ask, What do we want to improve? What are the learners' barriers? Does this modality address those better than others? When chosen purposefully and tied to outcomes, such tools move from being trendy tech to part of an effective learning system.

Pulling Things Together: A Straightforward Way to Choose and Blend Learning Methods

Choosing the right delivery method for a learning program—face-to-face, self-paced, or online—directly affects how participants engage with the content. Ensure the approach aligns with your audience's needs.

I have developed a straightforward framework that I regularly rely on when designing multi-format programs. It is not elaborate, but it ensures I remain focused during the planning process. The initial consideration is, What are learners expected to do, and in what context? It is followed by, Do they work from home? Are they out in the field? What's their schedule? What tools are they currently using? Is the content aligned with the learning objectives? Is there extraneous content? (*Avoid the common pitfall of presenting excessive content without clear purpose.*) Does the organization have an LMS? What do I need to track to measure training effectiveness and behavior change? What devices are learners using to engage with the content?

It's important to design courses to provide good used experience on mobile devices. This helps you to determine the best modalities to meet learners where they are, rather than expecting them to adapt to your delivery modality.

So, instead of defaulting to the shiniest new tech or the trendiest theory, I focus on listening—what are the real barriers impacting performance, what excites learners, what slows them down? Sometimes it's bandwidth issues, other times it's confidence, or just a hectic schedule. My goal is to identify the pain points and the sweet spots where learning actually fits and feels relevant.

A few key practices are maintained: using a consistent tone and voice across formats, reintroducing earlier examples for familiarity, and consistently connecting content to real-life applications. Learning reinforcement methods such as tip sheets, infographics, or short videos are integrated. Learners should understand how the material relates to their job responsibilities.

Finally, a well-structured multimodal learning architecture doesn't rely solely on technology or frameworks—it evolves through observation and iteration. Regular feedback from learners is crucial: Are they using the resources? What do they find most useful? Are the learning interventions translating into confident, capable performance on the job? These questions guide refinement and help ensure that the learning strategy remains agile and responsive to actual needs.

Incorporating mechanisms for ongoing assessment such as quick pulse check surveys, informal check-ins, and learner analytics from digital platforms provides actionable data insights. This evidence-based approach supports continuous improvement, allowing instructional designers to pivot quickly if a particular modality isn't resonating or if new challenges emerge in the workplace.

Ultimately, the priority is to create learning experiences that reflect the realities of the modern workforce. By blending the right mix of instructional design strategies, innovative tools, practical delivery methods, and a deep understanding of learner needs, organizations can foster environments where people not only acquire new skills but feel empowered to apply them, turning learning from a mere event into habit-forming performance improvement.

CHAPTER 10

Evaluating Training Effectiveness

Introduction

Learning analytics has become a critical tool in the modern instructional designer's toolkit. By systematically tracking learner progress and outcomes, instructional designers, educators, L&D professionals, and organizations can identify areas for growth, implement targeted improvements, and enhance the effectiveness of learning and development programs.

Leveraging Data for Real-Time Improvement

Organizations and academic institutions can now embed interactive scenario-based learning with xAPI statements tied to learning objectives and course materials throughout eLearning or online courses. This enables real-time tracking of learner progress and engagement, allowing for immediate adjustments to content that address knowledge gaps.

Evaluation as an Integral Process

Evaluation is no longer an afterthought to be considered at the end of training. Instead, it is integrated into the instructional design process and business case development. By using models such as ADDIE, SAM, Agile instructional, and The New World Kirkpatrick's Model, instructional designers can design, deliver, and assess learning experiences that demonstrate measurable impact. This approach ensures that training is not just engaging, but also effective, meeting or exceeding the expectations of learners and stakeholders alike.

Reimagining Evaluation

This chapter invites readers to reimagine how learning evaluation is approached. Rather than treating evaluation as a post-mortem report or simply a matter of scoring 80% or above on a posttest to receive a certificate of completion, evaluation planning should be an integral step in the instructional design process. It should be considered during storyboarding, not after the fact.

Modern Tools for Enhanced Outcomes

With modern learning analytics powered by AI and xAPI statements, learner analytics dashboards, and data design, educators and instructional designers can enhance learner outcomes, optimize learning design, and improve performance.

Types of Learner Analytics

Learning analytics can initially appear overwhelming, especially when considered as a single, all-encompassing concept (Siemens & Baker, 2012; Ferguson, 2012). To bring clarity and highlight the distinct advantages each approach offers, it is helpful to examine the four main types of learning analytics. Understanding these categories allows instructional designers and educators to discern the unique purpose and value of each type of learner analysis.

Descriptive Analytics: What happened?

Descriptive analytics centers on summarizing historical learner data. This includes metrics such as completion rates, quiz scores, and hours spent engaging with lesson content. For example, a descriptive analysis might reveal that 80% of learners completed the HIPAA module within 30 days. Such findings are crucial for compliance reporting and for identifying patterns and trends in learner behavior.

Diagnostic Analytics: Why did it happen?

Diagnostic analytics goes a step further by exploring the underlying reasons for learner performance or disengagement. For instance, analysis may show that learners who skipped didactic content subsequently failed a scenario-based case study. This type of analytics is invaluable for pinpointing gaps in engagement, such as low participation rates, and for aligning resources to ensure that learning materials and performance support match learners' needs and job requirements.

Predictive Analytics: What is likely to happen?

Predictive analytics focuses on using existing learner data to project future performance and outcomes. By carefully analyzing patterns in learner behavior and achievement, instructional designers can identify potential challenges before they become significant obstacles. This approach enables proactive intervention, allowing educators to tailor learning experiences to better meet individual needs and foster greater success.

One of the key strategies in predictive analytics is leveraging data patterns, such as quiz results and engagement metrics, to forecast which learners may be at risk. For instance, if analysis reveals that 20% of learners are consistently showing low engagement and poor quiz scores, these individuals are likely at risk of failing the posttest. Recognizing these trends early on allows educators to implement targeted interventions that address specific learning gaps.

In practical terms, predictive analytics supports adaptive learning strategies. For example, learners who do not pass a quiz can be directed through branching interactions that guide them back to lesson content aligned with the quiz's learning objectives. This process helps learners revisit and strengthen areas where they need improvement, ultimately enhancing overall performance.

Prescriptive Analytics: What should we do about it?

Prescriptive analytics moves beyond simply reporting data and predictions; instead, it provides actionable recommendations for specific interventions designed to improve learning outcomes. This type of analytics is focused on determining the best course of action based on learners' needs and performance data.

- **Targeted Recommendations**: Prescriptive analytics suggests specific learning interventions, such as assigning additional practice scenarios or activities to learners who demonstrate low performance. For example, learners struggling with clinical documentation may be assigned extra practice exercises to reinforce their skills.

- **Use Case:** By implementing these targeted recommendations, instructional designers and educators can move from reporting learner performance to actively driving performance improvement and supporting learners in achieving their objectives.

Introduction to SCORM and xAPI

The Sharable Content Object Reference Model (SCORM), introduced in 2000 by the Advanced Distributed Learning (ADL) Initiative, established technical standards for eLearning content to communicate with learning management systems (LMS). SCORM enabled the reporting of several basic metrics, including completion status, pass/fail results, time spent on content, and assessment scores. While these metrics remain useful, they offer only a limited perspective on learner performance, capturing a narrow snapshot rather than the full learning journey.

The Need for Richer Data in Modern L&D

Contemporary performance-based learning and development programs demand more comprehensive data. Today, organizations seek to understand not only whether learners completed activities, but also how they interacted with content, how they applied skills in simulations, which resources they accessed during and after learning, and whether these actions contributed to learning outcomes. One critical question is whether the learning experience accurately reflects actions required on the job. This evolving need for detailed analytics led to the development of the Experience API (xAPI), a standard designed to link learning activities more closely to performance outcomes.

xAPI: Advancing Learner Performance Tracking

The Experience Application Programming Interface (xAPI), also known as Tin Can API, is a technology standard for collecting and analyzing learning data. xAPI allows for tracking of learner performance across diverse platforms, providing a much more granular understanding of learning activities. Unlike SCORM, which focuses primarily on completion, time spent, and assessment scores within an LMS, xAPI broadens the scope of learning analytics by enabling the tracking of nearly any learning activity, online or offline. This includes mobile apps, simulations, virtual reality experiences, and even activities such as reading an article. By capturing these interactions, xAPI helps identify where interventions are needed, assesses the effectiveness of learning activities, and supports enhancements to the overall learning experience, extending beyond the boundaries of the LMS.

Learning Record Store (LRS) and xAPI Statements

xAPI data is stored in a Learning Record Store (LRS), a system that collects, stores, and retrieves learning experience data in the form of xAPI statements. Each xAPI statement follows an Actor-Verb-Object structure, providing detailed records of learner interactions. For example:

- **Actor**: Carly or learner ID
- **Verb**: completed
- **Object**: Introduction to Medical Terminology Course

Examples of xAPI Statements in Healthcare Administration

The following table presents examples of learning events and corresponding xAPI statements from a Doctor of Health Administration program. These demonstrate xAPI's ability to capture detailed data regarding learner interactions across various competencies, such as policy analysis, financial management, quality improvement, and strategic planning.

Learning Event	xAPI Statement
Quiz attempt	"Dorothy attempted The Art of Negotiation Quiz 1."
Quiz question answered	"Dorothy answered Question 4 correctly in The Art of Negotiation Quiz 1."
Video viewed	"Dorothy watched Introduction to Health Informatics video."
Resource accessed	"Dorothy downloaded 'SBAR on Inpatient Medical Unit'.pdf."
Discussion forum	"Dorothy posted a reply to Ethical Use of AI in Healthcare Discussion Forum."
Simulation interaction	"Dorothy interacted with Virtual Patient Assessment Triage Simulation

Table 10.1 xAPI Statements

Pro Tip: xAPI (Experience API) opens up powerful possibilities for tracking learning beyond traditional LMS platforms. To learn more, please visit. https://xapi.com/ or Advanced Digital Learning at adlnet.gov/projects/xapi/

Visualizing Learner Performance with Tableau

Data without visualization is like a map without landmarks—you have information, but struggle to see the patterns and pathways. While xAPI and Learning Record Stores provide the data infrastructure for modern learning analytics, business intelligence tools like Tableau transform raw data into actionable insights through interactive visualizations. As an instructional designer or L&D professional, Tableau enables you to move beyond static reports to dynamic dashboards that reveal learner behavior patterns, identify at-risk learners, and demonstrate training impact to stakeholders (Few, 2013; Knaflic, 2015).

Tableau has become the industry standard for learning analytics visualization because it connects directly to Learning Record Stores, can process millions of xAPI statements, and creates interactive dashboards that update in real-time. Unlike Excel charts or PowerPoint slides, Tableau dashboards allow stakeholders to filter data, drill down into specific cohorts, and explore trends at their own pace. For healthcare education programs, this means faculty can monitor DNP learner clinical hour completion, track DHA learner engagement with financial management simulations, or identify which AACN Essentials require additional instructional support, all from a single, interactive dashboard.

Tableau excels at transforming the four types of learning analytics into visual stories. For descriptive analytics, create completion rate dashboards showing which modules have the highest drop-off points. For diagnostic analytics, build heat maps revealing when learners disengage—perhaps discovering that 70% of quiz failures occur after 8 PM, suggesting fatigue or competing priorities. For predictive analytics, use trend lines and forecasting to identify learners at risk of not completing the program before the deadline. For prescriptive analytics, design dashboards that automatically flag learners who need intervention and suggest specific learning resources based on their performance patterns (Siemens & Long, 2011; Daniel, 2015).

Practical Tableau Applications in Healthcare Education

Consider these real-world scenarios where Tableau dashboards drive better learning outcomes. An assistant professor uses Tableau to track engagement with conflict resolution and negotiation case studies. When the dashboard reveals that learners who watch supplemental videos score 15% higher on conflict resolution assignments, faculty add more video content and redesign the module to promote video engagement. Another healthcare organization uses Tableau to demonstrate ROI on their training investment, showing executives a dashboard with before-and-after performance metrics, cost per learner, and time-to-competency across different training modalities.

Visualization Type	Use Case	Learning Analytics Question Answered
Bar Charts	Compare completion rates across modules or cohorts	Which courses have the highest/lowest completion rates?
Line Graphs	Track learner progress over time	Is engagement increasing or decreasing throughout the semester?
Heat Maps	Identify peak engagement times and content hot spots	When are learners most active? Which content gets the most interaction?
Scatter Plots	Correlate assessment scores with engagement metrics	Do learners who spend more time on content score higher?
Funnel Charts	Visualize learner progression through program stages	Where in the learning pathway are students dropping out?
Box Plots	Show score distributions and identify outliers	How much variation exists in learner performance?
Geographic Maps	Display learner locations for distributed programs	Where are our online learners located? Do regional patterns exist?
Dashboard Filters	Enable stakeholders to explore data by cohort, date, or demographics	How does this year's cohort compare to last year's?

Table 10.2: Common Tableau Visualizations for Learning Analytics

Best Practices for Learning Analytics Dashboards

Creating effective Tableau dashboards requires more than technical skills, it demands understanding your audience and their decision-making needs. Start by identifying the key questions stakeholders need answered: Are learners completing the program? Are they mastering critical competencies? Is the training producing measurable performance improvement? Then design dashboards that answer these questions at a glance, using the principle of 'progressive disclosure' show summary metrics prominently, then allow users to drill down for details (Cairo, 2016; Knaflic, 2015).

Follow these evidence-based design principles: Use color strategically to highlight important information, not to decorate. Stick to 3-5 colors maximum, reserving red for alerts and green for success. Avoid pie charts when comparing more than three categories, bar charts are easier to interpret accurately. Include context by showing benchmarks, targets, or historical comparisons so stakeholders understand whether performance is improving. Add filters that allow users to view data by relevant segments, cohort, program, clinical site, or time period. Most importantly, design for your audience: executive dashboards should focus on high-level trends and ROI, while faculty dashboards need granular detail for individual learner interventions (Few, 2013).

Tableau integrates seamlessly with Learning Record Stores through database connections or API integrations, allowing you to visualize xAPI statements directly. When connected to your LRS, Tableau can automatically refresh dashboards daily or even hourly, ensuring stakeholders always see current data. For healthcare education programs managing competency-based education, this real-time visibility is transformative—faculty can intervene with struggling learners immediately rather than discovering problems weeks later through traditional grade reports. Combined with the evaluation models discussed in the next section, Tableau provides the visual evidence needed to demonstrate training effectiveness and justify continued investment in learning and development programs.

> *Training has no value unless what is learned get applied on the job, and the subsequent on-the-job performance contributes to key organizational outcomes.*
>
> *Dr. Jim Kirkpatrick & Dr. Wendy Kirkpatrick*

Training Evaluation Models

One of the most significant and most difficult aspects of training is to prove that that your intervention was effective and worth the investment. It is no longer enough for training to be "liked" by participants, it must be proven to be effective in improving job performance. If not, it has no value. Let's explore three models of evaluating training programs.

The New World Kirkpatrick® Model

Kirkpatrick' Four Levels of Training Evaluation was developed in the 1950s and is considered the gold standard for training assessment. However, today's digital learning strategies must facilitate rapid workplace technological advances, immersive learning experiences with real world context, requiring a revised approach to measure training effectiveness. The shift to the New World Kirkpatrick® Model marks an important revolution in how learning and development effectiveness is measured. While the original model began with measuring learner reactions to the training, the new model (Kirkpatrick & Kirkpatrick, 2016) takes a different approach by identifying the results, focusing on leading indication and desired outcomes and work backwards to ensure L&D programs are effective.

Instead of treating the four levels as a hierarchy or afterthought, the enhanced framework encourages designers and L&D professionals to start with Level 4 (Results). By building backwards from desired outcomes, every decision in design, delivery, and evaluation supports real-world performance.

For example, if a healthcare organization aims to improve patient satisfaction scores, L&D programs are designed with this outcome in mind from the beginning. Evaluation then focuses on whether these scores improve after the training is completed. This process transforms evaluation from a checklist into a strategic, ongoing improvement process that drives both learner success and organizational goals.

Key enhancements to the Kirkpatrick Model include:

- **Begin with Results**: The New World Kirkpatrick® Model emphasizes beginning at Level 4, asking, "What organizational outcome are we trying to influence?" Working backwards to ensure all forms or evaluation aligns with that outcome.

- **Building a Chain of Evidence**: Stitching together storylines and data across all levels to build a compelling narrative. A "chain of evidence" that connects reaction, learning, behavior, and results.

- **Focus on Relevance and Reinforcement:** Level 1 (Reaction) now includes *relevancy as a strong predictor of application rather than mere likeability*. It also recommends formative "pulse checks" rather than waiting until course completion for feedback.

- **Increased emphasis on confidence and commitment** in Level 2 (Learning) viewing these as early indicators of behavior change.

Legacy Evaluation Method	New World Kirkpatrick® Model
Evaluations start with learner satisfaction	Shift to metrics that matter—begin with intended outcomes, Level 4 (Results) and align backwards
Feedback collected post completion	Pulse surveys and relevancy checks can be used in real time to make adjustments during the learning process.
Learning measured only by test scores	Include confidence measures (such as self-assessed certainty levels) and learner commitment (tracked by LMS analytics) to assess student engagement (e.g., time invested) and performance.
Evaluation as an afterthought	Build a chain of evidence that connects design decisions to learner, team and organizational outcomes
Chapters treated as sequential	Design evaluation as an integrated, continuous process aligned with xAPI tracking, dashboards, and iterative improvement.

Table 10.3: Legacy Evaluation Methods vs New World Kirkpatrick® Model of Evaluation

While the New World Kirkpatrick® Model remains the most widely used framework in eLearning, it is not the only option. The **Phillips ROI Model** adds a financial lens to Kirkpatrick's framework, while **Brinkeroff's Success Case Method (SCM)** takes a qualitative, case-based approach. Each model offers unique strengths and limitations, and in practice, instructional designers often find value in combing them to assess training effectiveness and demonstrating value to stakeholders.

Phillips ROI Model

The Phillips ROI model builds on Kirkpatrick by adding a fifth level of evaluation: Return on Investment (ROI). In his book, Return on Investment in Training and Performance Improvement, Jack Phillips (1997; see also

Phillips & Phillips, 2016) highlighted the importance of measuring the 'return on investment' for training programs by evaluating effectiveness on five levels. The key question answered by using the Phillips ROI Model is what is the monetary value of the training compared its cost?

1. **Reaction**: identifies learner satisfaction with the training.

2. **Learning:** determines knowledge or skills acquired from the training.

3. **Application:** examines whether learners transfer skills learned to their job roles.

4. **Impact:** assesses the influence of the training program on business outcomes (e.g. changes in customer satisfaction scores).

5. **Return on Investment (ROI)**: compares the monetary benefits resulting from the training to its cost, expressing the return on investment.

The Phillips ROI Model is widely used for assessing the business impact of training and return on investment (ROI), but it has certain limitations. Evaluating business impact often involves extensive data collection and analysis, and isolating the effects of training on performance can be challenging, as external factors such as policy changes or market conditions may also influence outcomes.

Brinkeroff's Success Case Method (SCM)

Created by Robert Brinkerhoff (2003), the Success Case Method (SCM) identifies the most and least successful cases within your L&D programs and studies them in detail.Brinkerhoff's Success Case Method (SCM) offers a practical, story-driven approach to evaluating training effectiveness. Rather than seeking to measure every participant's outcome, SCM focuses on identifying and analyzing the most and least successful cases within a training cohort. Through interviews, surveys, and qualitative data, instructional designers uncover what worked, what didn't, and why. This method provides rich, contextual insights that numbers alone can't capture, making it especially valuable for uncovering the real-world impact of training initiatives and guiding future improvements. While SCM is typically associated with learning and development programs, it is also applicable for analyzing a wide range of business changes, including technology acquisitions and the implementation of process improvement strategies. Kirkpatrick's evaluation model relies on quantitative approaches, including surveys and assessment data, to measure the effectiveness of learning programs. In contrast, SCM adopts qualitative methods, generating narratives from discussions conducted with a small group, typically two to six—of participants affected by the learning program. The underlying premise is that learning programs often result in various levels of success and failure; analysis focuses on identifying significant successful outcomes and failures, then documenting these with supporting evidence. Stakeholders use these findings to inform the development of future learning programs.

All three methods have their benefits and drawbacks, as an instructional designer I utilize all three methods of evaluation, sometimes using one to address the limitations of another. Careful evaluation is essential to the instructional design process because it directly supports our ability to improve performance, meet organizational goals, and achieve meaning change through learning. Regardless of which evaluation method or combination you use, the goal is to assess your L&D projects for effectiveness and impact. The ultimate aim is for participants to apply what they've learned to improve job performance, thereby helping organizations achieve their intended change. When participants successfully apply new skills on the job, organizations are more likely to achieve meaningful improvements and reach strategic goals, demonstrating a direct link between performance goals and organizational success.

Conclusion

The integration of advanced learning analytics and robust evaluation models represents a transformative approach in instructional design, ensuring that learning and development programs not only deliver engaging content but also drive measurable improvements in job performance and strategic outcomes. By leveraging both quantitative methods such as those found in the Phillips ROI Model and Kirkpatrick's evaluation model and qualitative techniques like Brinkerhoff's Success Case Method, instructional designers can build a comprehensive understanding of program effectiveness. This holistic evaluation process supports ongoing organizational growth by informing future instructional design decisions and aligning learning initiatives with business objectives. Ultimately, the careful and continuous assessment of L&D programs fosters a culture of evidence-based improvement, enabling organizations to adapt swiftly to changing needs and maximize the impact of their learning investments.

CHAPTER 11

Designing for Performance Means Designing for All

Why Accessibility Matters

Meet Jennifer, a medical assistant gazing at an assessment on her laptop. She has spent the past hour trying to navigate a course module. The content is not difficult, but it's delivered as a scenario-based assessment in video format with no captions or transcript. Jennifer, a learner who has partial hearing loss, cannot access the content to complete the assessment as effortlessly as other learners. Meanwhile, Tony has encountered a different barrier, he uses his screen reader to navigate the same course and encounter images labeled figure 1.jpg and an interactive infographic that announces as clickable element. Stacy experiences challenges with the color-coded system that uses red and green to indicate correct and incorrect answers, these colors are hard to distinguish because she is color blind.

Color blindness, the most common type of vision deficiency, means individuals are unable to perceive colors as others do or may not see color at all according to the National Institutes of Health, National Eye Institute (2023). Individuals with both *protanopia*, a vision deficiency where shades of red look more green and less bright, and *deuteranopia*, where certain shades of green look more red, cannot distinguish the difference between red and green at all (National Eye Institute, 2023).

This isn't hyperbole. These scenarios represent 20% of learners, over 3.5 million learners nationwide, one in five learners enrolled in your courses who have disabilities, each facing barriers that are entirely preventable (Lowenthal & Lomellini, 2023; McAndrew et al., 2012; NCES, 2023). Even more alarming is the number of learners with disabilities could be even greater because these statistics only represent learners who *reported* having a disability (Lowenthal & Lomellini, 2023; McAndrew et al., 2012).

Here's the uncomfortable truth: Most eLearning and online experiences are designed for the imaginary average learner. The neurotypical learner—individuals "having a style of neurocognitive functioning that falls within the dominant societal standards of normal" (Dwyer, 2022; Walker, 2014). But what is normal? When we design for the fictional norms, we exclude millions of people from the learning experience. People whose education and job performance remains locked behind barriers we unintentionally build into our digital learning environments. Now here's another truth, one that encourages and empowers: Accessible design is good design for all learners. The video captions and transcripts that are essential for learners with special needs are also helpful for the learner who is working at her desk and can't turn on audio, or a learner who is viewing a training video in a noisy environment and needs to turn on captions to read the content instead of listening to the audio. High-contrast text helps both learners with poor vision and those with normal sight working in bright environments avoid eye strain. Apply WCAG standards to strike the right balance. A clear course navigation and alternative text (alt text) for images and graphics make content easy to find for screen reader users and help all learners navigate the course smoothly.

The Cost of Exclusion: Through the Lens of Corporate Education

Consider the following scenario: Your organization invests $500,000 in authoring and developing a comprehensive high-fidelity eLearning stroke certification course. It features dynamic graphics, engaging video content, active learning interactions, infographics, scenario-based assessments aligned with course competencies, and industry standards. Six months post-launch, you receive a complaint, the course is inaccessible to employees with disabilities. What would you do?

A. Retrofit the entire course at a cost that could exceed the original business case budget

B. Explain to your customers that updates are completed on a scheduled cycle and leave the course active until the next schedule review and update

C. Meet with the client to learn more about the complaint; review course design document and table of contents; identify all modules and screens containing videos, images, and audio; identify accessibility issues with media and colors, checking for missing captions, transcripts, unclear audio; and make updates to meet WCAG standards.

The answer is **C.** Unfortunately, this scenario is based on a real problem that occurs across academic institutions and corporations worldwide. Yet, it's completely avoidable. Let's explore how.

UDL and WCAG: Laying the Foundation

An essential element of my learning design strategy in both my roles in corporate education and higher education is knowing that Universal Design for Learning (UDL) principles and WCAG 2.1 Level AA compliance are essential foundational elements of effective and inclusive learning experiences. Just as a builder lays the foundation before building a house, it is just as important for educators, instructional designers, learning designers, and eLearning developers to embed these principles at the very beginning of conceptualizing an eLearning project.

The UDL Framework as Design DNA

Universal Design for Learning is a framework based on the science of how people learn based on evidence that can transform the approach to instructional and learning design. The three pillars for design multiple means of *engagement and motivation*, *representation*, and *action and expression* empowers learners with the autonomy and agency to drive their own learning experience and outcomes (CAST, 2024).

Multiple means of engagement and motivation moves beyond compliance to motivating and improving engagement for all learners Here are some examples:

- Designing role-based learning includes challenge-choice-consequence scenarios, providing autonomy in choosing their learning path and choice in their challenge level (e.g., novice to expert), authoring culturally competent content, implementing diversity in the images contained in content materials, authoring and designing learning content with a diverse audience of learners in mind.

- Create learning experiences to engage the learner with ADHD who needs frequent breaks, the working parent who only has 20 minutes a day to study, and the healthcare professional with competing priorities working in a high-pressure healthcare environment who only has 15 minutes a day to complete a list of mandatory compliance training.

- Ensure engaging microlearning moments that include short 2-to-5-minute videos, interactive PDFs, or 10-minute narrated slide-based learning nugget. A 3-to-5-minute podcast can provide multiple means of engagement that will meet diverse learner needs.

Multiple means of representation provides a richer sensory learning experience that helps improve comprehension for visual learners reading along with audio. Alternative text that describes images or adding closed-captions and downloadable transcripts can improve retention and comprehension for all learners.

Multiple means of action & expression ensure that content is not confined to a single format. The learner who struggles with a written presentation may excel when given the opportunity to create a video or PowerPoint presentation. A learner who may not have strong public speaking skills may excel when given the opportunity to present a written report. By offering options like, creating an infographic, video, narrated slide-based presentation, or providing multiple-choice assessment, case-based scenarios, and problem-based learning, you allow learners to demonstrate their true capabilities.

UDL provides the pedagogical framework, and WCAG 2.1 Level AA provides the technical specifications to make content accessible. Applying these guidelines is how we remove the barriers to learning.

The Performance Designer's Role in Accessibility

As an instructional designer, eLearning developer, and assistant professor of an online graduate degree program, I stand at the intersection of technology, and L&D. Every decision from course authoring tools, learning management systems, course design, color choices, screen design, images, alternative text, transcripts, navigation, assessment, video production, and editing will either create an inclusive and effective learning environment or create barriers. Reflecting on the scenario at the beginning of this chapter, I can influence whether Jennifer, Tony, and Stacy have access to learning opportunities or encounter obstacles in advancing, passing exams, or finishing their college degrees.

Accessibility and universal design for learning (UDL) aren't just about checklists or meeting minimum standards but about a mindset shift that must happen in higher education and corporate learning to proactively and strategically prioritize accessibility and inclusivity in digital learning environments and digital learning products that meet the needs of diverse learners. Accessibility and inclusion are more than special accommodation requiring a health provider's validation: It's about creating digital environments and learning solutions that benefit all learners. In a world where digital learning has become the primary pathway to education, workforce development and economic opportunity, every course that is not accessible to diverse learners is a closed door to human potential, reskilling and upskilling a highly trained healthcare workforce.

Core Accessibility Must-Haves

Visual Accessibility

- Scalable text with resizable fonts
- Use alternative (alt text) for all images
- High-contrast and color-contrast compliance

Auditory Accessibility

- Full transcripts of multimedia; when media contains multiple speakers, identify each speaker.

- Ensure transcripts and closed captioning on all video/audio are synchronized and accurate.

- When using text-to-speech or AI voiceover technology, opt for humanlike voiceover. Also ensure that the audio is not robotic and that all terms are pronounced correctly. Use phonetic spellings to help with pronunciations. Edit the VTT or SRT caption file for accuracy.

- For medical voiceover text-to-speech technology, it is essential that medical terms are pronounced correctly. Use phonetic spellings from a medical dictionary to help with phonetic spellings.

Navigation and Structure

- Provide clearly labeled navigation buttons.
- Ensure logically consistent navigation and course menu structures.
- Provide clear course maps and learner progress indicators.
- Enable keyboard accessibility (ensure course navigation for non-mouse users).

Cognitive Accessibility

- Chunk or segment content to reduce cognitive overload.
- Use plain language.
- Enforce consistence in the use of icons, colors, and design patterns.
- Design multiple ways of active engagement.

Interaction and Assessment

- Provide screen reader-friendly quizzes and simulations.
- Include accessible drag-and-drop or click-to-reveal alternatives (ability to use tab key to navigate the interactive element).
- Add time extensions and flexible assessment delivery.

Multimedia Accessibility: Captions, Transcripts, and Timestamps

Timestamps in Closed Captions

Timestamps serve multiple critical functions in accessible multimedia content, and require careful consideration based on use case and audience needs. Closed caption files such as WebVTT, SRT, and SCC must include timestamps for accurate syncing. Captions are dependent on timestamps for the following reasons:

- **Synchronization:** Ensures text appears precisely when words are spoken.
- **Cognitive processing:** Allows appropriate reading time for each caption.
- **Navigation:** Enables learners to jump to specific points.
- **Assistive technology:** Screen readers and other tools rely on timing data.
- **Learning pace:** Supports learners who need to pause and process information.
- **WCAG compliance:** Required for Success Criterion 1.2.2.

Captions

Captions provide more than a transcription of speech to text—they also describe significant visuals, identify speakers, indicate emphasis, and include educational annotations. These features support access for learners who are deaf or hard of hearing. Captions can also aid ESL learners by enhancing reading comprehension as they follow along. Additionally, captions are useful for individuals viewing video content in noisy or quiet environments, such as libraries or workplaces, to minimize disruption.

Beyond these applications, captions serve as a vital bridge for inclusive design, supporting not only compliance but also universal usability by enhancing attention, recall, and engagement for diverse audiences. Their presence encourages active learning strategies, such as note-taking and reviewing complex material, which can benefit learners with various cognitive styles. By integrating captions within multimedia, educators and designers cultivate flexible learning pathways that respect individual preferences, foster accessibility, and reinforce comprehension. Such thoughtful implementation underscores the importance of captions as an integral component of effective, equitable digital learning.

Transcripts and Timestamps: A More Nuanced Decision

However, as it pertains to transcripts, the decision to use timestamps is more nuanced. Unlike captions, the decision to include timestamps on transcripts depends on the intended use and format.

A common misconception in eLearning accessibility is that transcripts must contain timestamps to be WCAG compliant. However, according to the W3C Web Accessibility Initiative, timestamps should be included "only when useful" and that in many cases, including timestamps would be unnecessary clutter (Web Accessibility Initiative, 2024). This is important for learners using screen readers because screen readers announce each timestamp, which may cause disruption of the flow of content and the reading experience. Many screen reader users set their devices to read much faster than natural speech (University of San Francisco, 2024), allowing the device to consume transcript content more efficiently than listening to the original audio, but only when timestamps are not present to interrupt the process. For eLearning designers, clean, readable transcripts without timestamps for study and reference purposes is a best practice. Use timestamped transcripts only for interactive applications where learners need to navigate to specific points or subjects in the media. This approach provides advantages for a range of learners, including individuals with hearing impairments who require access to content, those without disabilities who may use transcripts as study aids, and screen reader users who rely on uninterrupted text flow. Timestamps are important and essential for video captions, helping learners quickly find a specific part in a video or audio track, identification of speaker, and makes the media searchable.

When evaluating the accessibility and usability of transcripts, consider the audience and the learning objectives. For instance, learners who benefit from reviewing material at their own pace may prefer not to have a timestamped transcript for easier reference and concentration. Meanwhile, timestamped transcripts are beneficial in settings where precise navigation or synchronization with media is required, such as in technical training or when referencing specific segments during group discussions. The choice should be guided by the specific context and user needs to maximize inclusivity and learning efficacy.

The Choice Before Us

Let's be honest with each other for a moment.

Tomorrow morning, you're going to open your laptop and work on a course. Maybe you're building a new module from scratch, revising last year's content, or creating an assessment. And in that moment, you face dozens of small decisions that feel insignificant: Should I add captions to this 3-minute video? Does this image really need alternative (alt text)? Is it worth the extra time to test keyboard navigation?

Here's what I need you to understand, those aren't small decisions. They're the difference between Jennifer completing her medical assistant certification or dropping out. Between Tony advancing in his career or hitting a wall he can't navigate around. Between Stacy demonstrating what she actually knows or being judged by an assessment that can't accurately measure her competence.

When you take the 15 minutes to write meaningful alt text for Tony, you're also helping the learner whose image didn't load on their spotty rural internet connection. When you add captions for Jennifer, you're improving comprehension for the ESL learner, the parent studying after midnight with a sleeping baby in the next room, and the professional reviewing content during their commute. Accessible design isn't extra work for a small population—it's better design for everyone.

The Ripple Effect of Your Decisions

Here's something they don't tell you in instructional design programs: Your work outlives you. That course you built three years ago? It's still running. Learners you'll never meet are still encountering the choices you made. The barriers you created—or the doors you opened—continue to affect people long after you've moved on to other projects.

I think about this constantly. Somewhere right now, a learner is trying to access content I designed years ago. Did I make choices that included them or excluded them? Did I take the extra time, or did I cut corners? Those decisions ripple forward in ways I'll never fully see.

But here's what I've learned after twenty-five years in this field: accessible design isn't separate from performance design. It's the fullest expression of it.

Think back to the beginning of this book. Performance design asks: What results must improve? What behaviors will produce those results? What barriers prevent those behaviors?

When we exclude learners through inaccessible design, we create the ultimate barrier to performance. The nurse who can't complete her certification because the videos lack captions never gets the chance to demonstrate the clinical behaviors we designed the training to develop. The manager who can't navigate the leadership course because it requires a mouse never learns the conflict resolution skills his team desperately needs. The technician who abandons the safety training because the cognitive load overwhelms her never applies the protocols that protect her colleagues.

Inaccessible design doesn't just fail individual learners. It fails the organizations counting on improved performance. It fails the patients, customers, and communities those organizations serve. Every barrier we create is a behavior that never changes, a result that never improves, a performance gap that never closes.

Every barrier we remove is the opposite: a learner who succeeds, a behavior that transfers, a result that matters.

Building Your Accessibility Practice

This doesn't happen overnight, and you don't have to master everything at once. Build your skills deliberately:

This week: Add captions to one video. Just one. Use auto-captioning if you need to, but then actually edit for accuracy. Notice how long it takes. Probably less time than you feared.

This month: Learn to write effective alternative text. Start noticing how other designers handle images—or don't. When you encounter "image1.jpg" as alt text, imagine that experience through a screen reader. Then commit to never doing that in your own work.

This quarter: Test your courses with assistive technology. Install a screen reader and navigate your course using only a keyboard. It will be uncomfortable at first. You'll discover problems you never knew existed. That discomfort is growth.

This year: Make accessibility a core competency, not an afterthought. Build it into your templates, storyboards, and quality checklists. Make it as automatic as checking for typos or aligning with learning objectives.

The Conversation You'll Have Someday

Imagine this: Five years from now, you're having coffee with a colleague. They mention a learner who sent a thank-you email—someone who finally completed their certification after struggling for years. Someone who said your course was the first one that actually worked for them. The captions were accurate. The navigation was intuitive. The assessments offered multiple ways to demonstrate competence.

For the first time, they weren't fighting the design just to access the content. They could focus on learning. They could focus on performance.

Those decisions you made—to add captions even when the deadline was tight, to test with a screen reader even when you were exhausted, to advocate for accessibility even when stakeholders questioned the effort—those decisions changed someone's trajectory.

That learner might become a nurse who provides compassionate care because she understands what it's like to face unnecessary barriers. A teacher who designs inclusive classrooms because he experienced inclusive learning firsthand. A leader who champions accessibility because someone once championed it for her.

This is your legacy. Not the courses you built, but the performance you enabled. The behaviors that changed. The results that improved. The doors that opened because you designed them to open for everyone.

Full Circle: Performance Design for All

We began this book with a simple but profound shift: from asking "What content should learners receive?" to asking "What results must improve, and what behaviors will produce them?"

That shift transforms everything, how we analyze needs, how we design solutions, how we measure success. It grounds our work in learning science, focuses our delivery through strategic microlearning, and accelerates our development with AI assistance.

But performance design is incomplete if it only works for some learners.

The four pillars of this book, learning science, microlearning, performance design, and AI-supported development, all point toward the same destination: learning experiences that actually change behavior in the real world. Accessible design ensures that destination is reachable by everyone.

When you reduce cognitive load, you help the learner with ADHD and the exhausted night-shift worker and the executive checking training between meetings. When you provide multiple means of engagement, you reach the visual learner and the auditory learner and the learner who needs to move while thinking. When you design for the edges, you improve the experience for the center.

Universal design isn't a constraint on performance design. It's performance design fully realized.

Your Next Step

Throughout this book, you've developed a comprehensive toolkit for designing learning that works. You understand how people learn and how to apply that science. You know how to analyze performance gaps, design targeted interventions, and measure behavior change. You can leverage microlearning strategically and co-design with AI responsibly.

But knowledge without action is just potential energy waiting to be released.

So here's my challenge to you: Close this book, open your current project, and find one barrier you can remove today. One image that needs alt text.

One video that needs captions. One assessment that could offer more flexibility. Just one.

Then tomorrow, find another one.

Accessible, performance-focused learning isn't built in a single heroic effort. It's built in a thousand small decisions, made consistently, over time. It's built by designers like you who understand that excellence means designing for all learners—not just the imaginary average one.

Jennifer is waiting to show you what she can do when barriers don't hold her back. Tony is ready to bring his full potential to your learning environment. Stacy is prepared to demonstrate mastery when your assessments actually measure what they're supposed to measure.

These learners are counting on you to design for their performance, not just their compliance.

Not someday. Today.

Design for Performance. Design for All.

Every learner who can't access your content is a performance gap you created. Every learner who can is proof that this work matters.

You have the knowledge. You have the tools. You have the framework. You understand learning science. You know how to design for behavior change. You can build microlearning that sticks and leverage AI that accelerates.

Now it's time to use all of it—for every learner who will ever encounter your work.

Design with intention. Design with science. Design with empathy.

Design for performance. Design for all.

The learners are waiting. Your next design decision starts now.

References

7taps. (n.d.). *Microlearning for sales enablement: Real estate case study.* https://www.7taps.com/case-study/how-to-empower-your-sales-team-with-microlearning-ditch-the-scripts

Alder, S. (2025, April 9). *What is healthcare regulatory compliance? 2025 update.* HIPAA Journal. https://www.hipaajournal.com/healthcare-regulatory-compliance/

Alharbi, A., Nurfianti, A., Mullen, R. F., McClure, J. D., & Miller, W. H. (2024). The effectiveness of simulation-based learning (SBL) on students' knowledge and skills in nursing programs: A systematic review. *BMC Medical Education, 24*(1), 1099. https://doi.org/10.1186/s12909-024-06080-z

Bandura, A. (1977). Social learning theory. Englewood Cliffs, NJ: Prentice Hall.

Brinkerhoff, R. O. (2003). The success case method: Find out quickly what's working and what's not. Berrett-Koehler Publishers.

CAST. (2024). *Universal Design for Learning Guidelines version 3.0.* https://udlguidelines.cast.org

Chen, Y., Lehmann, C. U., & Malin, B. (2024). Digital information ecosystems in modern care coordination and patient care pathways and the challenges and opportunities for AI solutions. *Journal of Medical Internet Research, 26*, e60258. https://doi.org/10.2196/60258

Clark, R. C., & Mayer, R. E. (2023). *E-Learning and the science of instruction: Proven guidelines for consumers and designers of multimedia learning.* John Wiley & Sons.

Cook, D. A., & Artino, A. R. (2016). Motivation to learn: An overview of contemporary theories. *Medical Education, 50*(10), 997–1014. https://doi.org/10.1111/medu.13074

Dávila Rubio, A. M. (2017). Wiggins, G., & McTighe, J. (2005) *Understanding by design* (2nd ed.). Alexandria, VA: Association for Supervision and Curriculum Development ASCD [Review of the book *Understanding by design*, by G. Wiggins & J. McTighe]. *Colombian Applied Linguistics Journal, 19*(1), 140–142. https://doi.org/10.14483/calj.v19n1.11490

Dwyer, P. (2022). The neurodiversity approach(es): What are they and what do they mean for researchers? *Human Development, 66*(2), 73–92. https://doi.org/10.1159/000523723

Ebbinghaus, H. (n.d.). *The forgetting curve.* https://www.eng.auburn.edu/current-students/documents/forgetting-curve.pdf

Ericsson, K. A., Krampe, R. T., & Tesch-Römer, C. (1993). The role of deliberate practice in the acquisition of expert performance. Psychological Review, 100(3), 363-406.

Ferguson, R. (2012). Learning analytics: Drivers, developments and challenges. International Journal of Technology Enhanced Learning, 4(5-6), 304-317. https://doi.org/10.1504/IJTEL.2012.051816

Few, S. (2013). Information dashboard design: Displaying data for at-a-glance monitoring (2nd ed.). Analytics Press.

Giovanelli, L., Rotondo, F., & Fadda, N. (2024). Management training programs in healthcare: Effectiveness factors, challenges and outcomes. *BMC Health Services Research, 24*(1), Article 904. https://doi.org/10.1186/s12913-024-11229-z

Goldhaber, N. H., Jacobs, M. B., Laurent, L. C., & Knight, R. (2024). Integrating clinical research into electronic health record workflows to support a learning health system. *JAMIA Open, 7*(2), ooae023. https://doi.org/10.1093/jamiaopen/ooae023

Hug, T. (2005). Micro learning and narration: Exploring possibilities of utilization of narrations and storytelling for the designing of "micro units" and didactical micro-learning arrangements. *Proceedings of Media in Transition 4*, MIT.

iSpring Solutions. (2025). *Just in time training: Definition, benefits, and examples.* https://www.ispringsolutions.com/blog/just-in-time-training

Jones, L. (2024, November 18). How to Create Scenario-Based Learning Experiences. *ThingLink.* https://www.thinglink.com/blog/how-to-create-scenario-based-learning-experiences/

Kapp, K. M., & Defelice, R. A. (2019). *Microlearning: Short and sweet.* Association for Talent Development.

Karpicke, J. D., & Blunt, J. R. (2011). Retrieval practice produces more learning than elaborative studying with concept mapping. Science (New York, N.Y.), 331(6018), 772–775. https://doi.org/10.1126/science.1199327

Kilmann. (2024). *Take the Thomas-Kilmann Conflict Mode Instrument (TKI) Take this assessment tool and discover which of the five conflict modes you might be using too much or too little… or just right.* Kilmann Diagnostics. https://kilmanndiagnostics.com/overview-thomas-kilmann-conflict-mode-instrument-tki/

Kirkpatrick, J. D., & Kirkpatrick, W. K. (2016). Kirkpatrick's four levels of training evaluation. ATD Press.

Knaflic, C. N. (2015). Storytelling with data: A data visualization guide for business professionals. Wiley.

Lee, T. S., Kuo, M. H., Borycki, E. M., & Yunyong, D. (2011). Critical success factors for implementing healthcare e-learning. *Studies in Health Technology and Informatics, 164*, 64–68.

Li, Y., Zhang, X., Wang, S., & Liu, H. (2025). Evaluation of the effectiveness of standardized training for new nurses using the

Kirkpatrick model: An observational study. *Medicine, 104*(23), e39127. https://doi.org/10.1097/MD.0000000000039127

Lowenthal, P. R., & Lomellini, A. (2023). Accessible online learning: A preliminary investigation of educational technologists' and faculty members' knowledge and skills. *TechTrends, 67*, 384–392. https://doi.org/10.1007/s11528-022-00790-1

Mahdavi Ardestani, S. F., Adibi, S., Golshan, A., & Sadeghian, P. (2023). Factors influencing the effectiveness of e-learning in healthcare: A fuzzy ANP study. *Healthcare (Basel, Switzerland), 11*(14), 2035. https://doi.org/10.3390/healthcare11142035

Mostrady, A., Sanchez-Lopez, E., & Gonzalez-Sanchez, A. F. (2024). Microlearning and its Effectiveness in Modern Education: A Mini Review. *Acta Pedagogia Asiana, 4*(1), 33–42. https://doi.org/10.53623/apga.v4i1.496

McAndrew, P., Farrow, R., & Cooper, M. (2012). Adapting online learning resources for all: Planning for professionalism in accessibility. *Research in Learning Technology, 20*(4), 345–361. https://doi.org/10.3402/rlt.v20i0.18699

McDade, S. (2023). Case-based patient scenario learning activity on medication administration. *Journal of Nursing Education, 62*(1), 63–64. https://doi.org/10.3928/01484834-20221109-09

McGee, R. G., Wark, S., Mwangi, F., et al. (2024). Digital learning of clinical skills and its impact on medical students' academic performance: A systematic review. *BMC Medical Education, 24*, 1477. https://doi.org/10.1186/s12909-024-06471-2

Monib, W. K., Qazi, A., & Apong, R. A. (2025). Microlearning beyond boundaries: A systematic review and a novel framework for improving learning outcomes. *Heliyon, 11*(2), e41413. https://doi.org/10.1016/j.heliyon.2024.e41413

Murre, J. M. J., & Dros, J. (2015). Replication and analysis of Ebbinghaus' forgetting curve. *PLoS ONE, 10*(7), e0120644. https://doi.org/10.1371/journal.pone.0120644

National Center for Education Statistics. (2023). *Fast facts: Students with disabilities (60).* U.S. Department of Education, Institute of Education Sciences. https://nces.ed.gov/fastfacts/display.asp?id=60

National Eye Institute. (n.d.). *Types of color vision deficiency.* https://www.nei.nih.gov/learn-about-eye-health/eye-conditions-and-diseases/color-blindness/types-color-vision-deficiency

Phillips, J. J. (1997). Return on investment in training and performance improvement programs. Gulf Publishing Company.

Phillips, P. P., & Phillips, J. J. (2016). Handbook of training evaluation and measurement methods (4th ed.). Routledge.

Siemens, G. (2005). Connectivism: A learning theory for the digital age. International Journal of Instructional Technology and Distance Learning, 2(1), 3-10.

Siemens, G., & Baker, R. S. J. d. (2012). Learning analytics and educational data mining: Towards communication and collaboration. In Proceedings of the 2nd International Conference on Learning Analytics and Knowledge (pp. 252-254). ACM. https://doi.org/10.1145/2330601.2330661

Kilmann. (2024). *Take the Thomas-Kilmann Conflict Mode Instrument (TKI) Take this assessment tool and discover which of the five conflict modes you might be using too much or too little... or just right.* Kilmann Diagnostics. https://kilmanndiagnostics.com/overview-thomas-kilmann-conflict-mode-instrument-tki/

upGrad Enterprise. (n.d.-b). The Workforce Wishlist 2025: United States of America | UpGrad Enterprise. https://www.upgrad-enterprise.com/reports/workforce-wishlist-the-usa-edition?05837444_page=2&utm_source=B2B2C_uGBwebsite&utm_medium=B2B2C_Instapage&utm_campaign=B2B2C_uGB

U.S. Bureau of Labor Statistics. (2025, August 28). Healthcare occupations. Occupational Outlook Handbook. https://www.bls.gov/ooh/healthcare/

Vygotsky, L. S. (1978). Mind in society: The development of higher psychological processes. Harvard University Press.

Walker, N. (2014). *Neurodiversity: Some basic terms & definitions.* Neuroqueer. https://neuroqueer.com/neurodiversity-terms-and-definitions/

Web Accessibility Initiative (WAI). (2024). Transcripts. In *Making audio and video media accessible.* World Wide Web Consortium (W3C). https://www.w3.org/WAI/media/

Wiggins, G., & McTighe, J. (2005). Understanding by Design (Expanded 2nd ed.). Association for Supervision and Curriculum Development. *(Chapters 1-3)*

Wroblewski, L. (2011). *Mobile First.* Ingram.

www.ingramcontent.com/pod-product-compliance
Lightning Source LLC
Chambersburg PA
CBHW060620130626
46555CB00002B/594